Cambridge Primary Reading Anthologies

4

Student's Book
with Online Audio

CAMBRIDGE
UNIVERSITY PRESS

Scope and Sequence

Unit 1 How do we express feelings?

	Genre	Key Words	Reading Strategy
Fiction *Homesick*	Realistic Fiction	mean, drag (v), shove (v), pretend, shocked, revenge, miss (v), grin (v)	Identifying Plot, Setting, and Characters
Nonfiction *Personality Test: Different Colors, Different Personalities!*	Personality Quiz	react, conflict (n), outgoing, concentrate (v), tolerant, fair, choice, cautious	Using Background Knowledge

Unit 2 What can space exploration teach us?

	Genre	Key Words	Reading Strategy
Fiction *Mars-to-Natalie*	Science Fiction	spacesuit, restrict, supervise, model (n), canyon, settlement, technical, impressed	Predicting from Pictures
Nonfiction *Exploring the Universe*	Informational Text on Space Exploration	lens, mirror, reflect, discover, astronomer, explosion, spiral (n), oval	Identifying the Main Idea and Details

Unit 3 Is technology good or bad?

	Genre	Key Words	Reading Strategy
Fiction *Charlie the Chorebot*	Science Fiction / Comedy Play	leftovers, nutritional, mess, promise (v), eliminate, feature (n), trial, scan (v)	Identifying the Main Idea and Details
Nonfiction *Low Technology— High Impact!*	Report on New Technologies	inventor, container, filter (v), germ, microscope, harm (v), connect, provide	Identifying the Main Idea and Details

Unit 4 How do we entertain ourselves?

	Genre	Key Words	Reading Strategy
Fiction *We're Going to Learn to Build Robots; If You Buy Me a Piano; Rules I Must Remember*	Poetry	wire (n), flame, saddle (n), kit, purchase (v), sore (adj), strum (v), selfie	Understanding the Meaning of Words from Context
Nonfiction *Let's Play*	Fun Fact Quiz / Historical Account	game console, dice (n), headset, flat, produce (v), video arcade, joystick, blindfold (v)	Making Inferences

Unit 5 What can history teach us?

	Genre	Key Words	Reading Strategy
Fiction *One Small Step*	Historical Fiction	decade, broadcast (n), newscaster, engine, recreate, powder, launch (n), experiment (n)	Identifying Cause and Effect
Nonfiction *The First Computer Programmer*	Biography of Inventor	code (n), replace, practical, talented, logical, influence (n), original, calculator	Identifying a Sequence of Events

Unit 6 Where does food come from?

	Genre	Key Words	Reading Strategy
Fiction *#AbuelaCooks*	Realistic Fiction	savory, feast (n), guru, crunchy, channel (n), organic, traditional, hashtag	Using Open Questions
Nonfiction *Are You Ready to Try … Meat Made in a Laboratory?*	Pro/Con Discussion of Food Technology	beef, protein, laboratory, cell, requirement, reproduce, lean (adj), predict	Identifying the Author's Purpose

Unit 7 Why is water important?

	Genre	Key Words	Reading Strategy
Fiction *The Nereids*	Greek Myth	in trouble, ashamed, horrified, maze, beneath, sink (v), fishermen, monument	Identifying a Sequence of Events
Nonfiction *Running Dry*	Environment Science Report	salt water, rod, rainwater, cistern, desalination, evaporate, liquid, cheap	Identifying Reasons and Evidence

Unit 8 How do numbers shape our lives?

	Genre	Key Words	Reading Strategy
Fiction *Meghan's Math Saves the Day!*	Graphic Novel	fraction, bother (v), slice (n), stuck, hold on, height, bend over, calculate	Identifying Plot, Characters, and Setting
Nonfiction *Measures, Measures, Everywhere!*	Fun Fact Article / Historical Account	length, weight, measurement, pace (n), metric system, equal to, scale, equator	Identifying Conclusions

Unit 9 What makes the natural world so amazing?

	Genre	Key Words	Reading Strategy
Fiction *The Secret of El Dorado*	Adventure Story	shiver (v), cave (n), hidden, legend, website, project (v), strict, diamond	Understanding Characters
Nonfiction *Under the Sea: Amazing Aliens from Earth*	Magazine Article on Marine Biology	mysterious, spine, shell, camouflage (n), mimic, predator, prey (n), twitch (v)	Understanding the Meaning of Words from Context

1 How do we express feelings?

Key Words

1 🎧 **Preview the Key Words.**
1.1

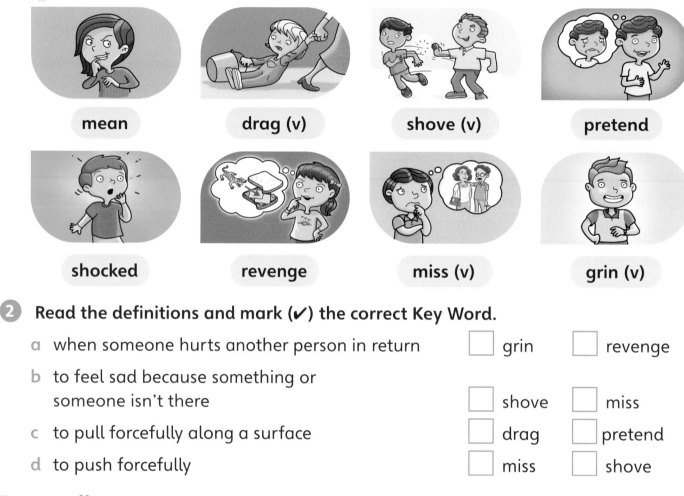

| mean | drag (v) | shove (v) | pretend |

| shocked | revenge | miss (v) | grin (v) |

2 **Read the definitions and mark (✔) the correct Key Word.**

a when someone hurts another person in return   ☐ grin   ☐ revenge

b to feel sad because something or
   someone isn't there   ☐ shove   ☐ miss

c to pull forcefully along a surface   ☐ drag   ☐ pretend

d to push forcefully   ☐ miss   ☐ shove

Pre-reading

3 **Look at the pictures on pages 5–7 and circle the correct options.**

What is the story about?	Where does it happen?	When does it take place?
a school trip	at a playground	now
a new boy at school	on a street	in the past
a frog in a lunchbox	in a school cafeteria	in the future

4 🎧 **Listen and read.**
1.2

Homesick

By Sarah Steinberg • Illustrated by Emmanuel Urueta

The cafeteria was loud. There were kids everywhere, many of them in little groups. It seemed like everyone was shouting. Did someone just throw an apple core at the garbage can? Jaime watched as the apple bounced off the side of the can and rolled onto the floor. He looked from the apple back to Liam. *Of course* it was him.

Liam was an eighth grader, and frankly, he was mean. Or, as Dylan liked to say, "He's a bully!" There he was, sitting at the cafeteria table—his dirty boots on the bench. Jaime looked over at Dylan and raised an eyebrow. Dylan raised his eyebrow back.

Jaime thought about how different school was here in Canada. Back home, in Bolivia, at his old school, nobody put their shoes on the bench like that. In La Paz, where Jaime was born, he wore a uniform to school every day. And he talked to grown-ups with respect. He wouldn't run through the hallways dragging his backpack behind him on the floor. Liam did that every day.

That was how he met Dylan. Liam was running through the hall, and when he passed Jaime, he shoved him hard, out of the way. For no reason! And Jaime fell. Then, suddenly there was Dylan, reaching his hand out to help him up.

"Are you OK?" Dylan asked him.

Jaime tried to pretend that he was, but he felt shocked and embarrassed. He let Dylan help him up.

"That guy Liam did the exact same thing to me last week, too," Dylan said.

After that, Jaime and Dylan walked to class together. And after school, they discovered they lived near one another. They were both in fourth grade. They liked talking about what they were learning in class and about Pokémon. And they both liked thinking about ridiculous ways to get revenge on Liam if he ever shoved them again. In one idea Jaime imagined, they put a frog into his lunchbox. They knew they wouldn't *really* do it, but it made them both feel better to talk about it.

Still, Jaime missed home. Arriving in Canada, Jaime was surprised to discover such a cold, harsh winter. At first, he loved it. But soon, he noticed how dark it was all the time. He missed the sun! Plus, it seemed like all the kids played hockey and he didn't. And sure, the grocery stores were enormous, but he missed the mango sellers on the streets of La Paz. That gave Jaime an idea. What if they hid great, big chunks of mangoes in Liam's shoes?

"Dylan, I have an idea!" Jaime said, "What if …"

But just as Jaime started talking, something caught Dylan's attention.

Dylan turned around, showing his back to Jaime.

Jaime felt like he'd been hit in the stomach. Back home, in Bolivia, turning your back on someone was considered extremely rude.

When Dylan turned back around, he could see something was wrong. By now, there weren't as many kids in the cafeteria, and it wasn't so loud anymore.

"What's wrong, Jaime?" Dylan said. "You look really upset."

"Do you still want to be friends?" Jaime asked sadly, looking down at the tabletop.

"Of course I do!"

"But you turned your back on me."

"So?"

"At home, if you turn your back on someone, it's like spitting in their face!"

"Oh!" Dylan said. "I didn't know that. I'm sorry."

It was nice of Dylan to apologize, but Jaime still felt sad. It was hard to live in a place where you don't know the customs, and you feel like you don't belong. He couldn't ask everyone to learn his rules.

"What's wrong?" asked Dylan.

"I don't know," Jaime said. "I guess I just miss home."

Dylan nodded. "I've been homesick before. You know what helped?

Talking about it! When I was homesick at camp, I told my counselors about it, and ..."

"Counselors?" Jaime asked.

"Yeah, my camp counselors, at summer camp! It's a sleepaway camp, and it's awesome!"

"Really?"

"Yeah! Tell me what you're homesick for, and then I'll tell you all about camp! And maybe this summer we can go together. That would be awesome!"

Jaime grinned. He still felt a little sad, but he also felt excited. The excitement that comes with knowing you made a good friend, and that sometime soon, you'll do something fun together.

Key Words

1 **Read the clues. Complete the crossword puzzle with the Key Words.**

Across

3 very selfish and unkind to others
4 unpleasantly surprised because of something unexpected

Down

1 to make believe or give a false appearance
2 to express pleasure by curving the lips upward

Comprehension

2 **Mark (✔) two types of revenge Jaime and Dylan thought about.**

☐ putting a fish in Liam's backpack
☐ placing a frog in Liam's lunchbox

☐ putting chunks of mangoes in Liam's shoes
☐ placing a lizard in Liam's locker

3 **Read and circle D (Dylan), J (Jaime), or L (Liam).**

a He invited his friend to summer camp.   D   J   L
b He threw an apple core at the garbage can. D   J   L
c He misses his hometown.   D   J   L
d He thought about putting mangoes in shoes. D   J   L
e He turned his back on his friend.   D   J   L
f He was mean and a bully.   D   J   L

4 **Answer the questions.**

a **Where** is Jaime from? _____

b **How** does Jaime feel about being in a different country? _____
_____

c **Why** did he get upset when Dylan turned his back on him? _____
_____

d **What** did Liam do to Dylan and Jaime? _____
_____

Digging Deeper

5 🔊 **Complete the story map.**

back	enjoys	Dylan	excited	cafeteria	fourth
fun	boy	upset	Bolivia	mean	Jaime

a **Main character:** A _____ named _____ from _____. He's in _____ grade.

b **Setting:** At the school _____.

c **Beginning:** He thinks Liam is _____. But he _____ being with his friend _____.

d **Middle:** He feels _____ because Dylan turns his _____ on him.

e **End:** He feels _____ because he'll do _____ things with Dylan.

6 Do you think bullies are usually happy people? Why or why not?

_____

_____

Personalization

7 **Imagine you are away from home.**

a How do you feel? Mark (✔) three feelings.

☐ happy   ☐ upset   ☐ sad   ☐ angry

☐ nervous   ☐ scared   ☐ excited   ☐ relaxed

b Who do you miss the most?

_____

_____

c What two things do you miss the most?

_____

_____

How do we express feelings?

Key Words

1 **Preview the Key Words.**
1.3

react

conflict (n)

outgoing

concentrate (v)

tolerant

fair

choice

cautious

2 **Read the glossary entries and circle the correct Key Word.**

a *adjective* treating everyone in the same way   choice   fair

b *noun* a situation where people disagree   conflict   cautious

c *verb* to pay attention   react   concentrate

d *verb* to do something because something
   else happened   tolerant   react

Pre-Reading

3 **What do you know about personality tests? Complete the graphic organizer.**

What I Know	What I Want to Know
_____	_____
_____	_____
_____	_____

4 **Listen and read.**
1.4

Personality Test:
Different Colors, Different Personalities!

By Susana Ramírez Félix

Do you want to know more about yourself? Take this quick personality test! At the end, you will find out what color matches your personality.

Directions: Read and choose the option that best describes you.

1 When the teacher assigns a task in class, I …

- ⚪ am fine finishing last.
- ⚫ finish as soon as I can. I don't like finishing last.
- ⚪ get upset if I don't finish first.
- ⚫ try to work quickly, but I am fine if I don't finish first.

2 When I have to work with others, I …

- ⚫ prefer to work in a big group.
- ⚫ prefer to work in a small group so that everyone can participate.
- ⚪ have to be the group leader.
- ⚫ don't like it very much. I prefer to work alone.

3 When I receive suggestions from my teacher, I …

- ⚪ don't know how to react.
- ⚫ get worried and talk to the teacher after class.
- ⚪ listen, but I don't worry about it too much.
- ⚫ listen carefully and I ask questions.

4 When I have a problem with a classmate, I …

- ⚪ talk with a teacher, relative, or friend about it.
- ⚫ talk with him or her and try to solve the problem.
- ⚪ never have problems with a classmate. I get along well with all of them.
- ⚫ don't talk to anyone about it. I try to avoid conflict.

5 When a classmate is sad or worried, I …

- ⚪ tell a joke and try to make him or her laugh.
- ⚫ try to comfort him or her.
- ⚪ talk with him or her and see how I can help.
- ⚫ respect his or her privacy and I don't ask what's wrong.

6 Before taking an exam, I feel ...

- very relaxed.
- extremely worried.
- a little bit worried.
- comfortable.

7 When I do homework, I ...

- sometimes do not finish it.
- usually wait until someone tells me to do it.
- do it whenever I want to, but I always do it.
- do it as soon as I get home.

8 After finishing my homework, I ...

- don't worry about putting it away.
- put everything away when my mom or dad tells me to.
- put everything away before I go to bed.
- immediately put everything away.

9 I feel more comfortable when I ...

- don't make plans. I don't like routines!
- follow a flexible schedule, but I don't like to arrive late.
- follow my own routine. I don't like anyone to tell me what to do.
- follow a set routine all the time.

10 When I have free time, I prefer to play ...

- with a big group of friends.
- with one good friend.
- with a small group of friends.
- by myself.

11 When I meet a new classmate or neighbor, I ...

- tell a joke or funny story to help him or her feel comfortable.
- ask questions to get to know him or her.
- introduce myself immediately and talk about myself.
- wait until he or she introduces him or herself.

12 If I have the chance to help others, I ...

- only help when someone asks me to do it.
- do everything I can. I love to help people.
- offer to help because I have lots of good ideas.
- do not offer to help unless it's an emergency.

13 When I feel sad or worried, I ...

- talk about it with anyone who will listen.
- share my feelings with my parents or my friends.
- sometimes talk about it, but I can usually solve the problem myself.
- sometimes write about it, but I usually don't tell anyone.

14 If a classmate is telling a long, boring story, I ...

- ⚪ don't pay attention and start talking to another friend.
- ⚫ try to listen until the end of the story.
- ⚪ gently interrupt him or her and ask a question.
- ⚫ remain quiet but start drawing or writing in my notebook.

15 When I give a presentation in front of my class, I ...

- ⚪ feel relaxed. I'm not worried. It will be fine.
- ⚫ get nervous. I want my classmates and teacher to like it.
- ⚪ get excited. I love to give presentations!
- ⚫ feel confident. I prepare and practice, so it will be fine.

Now, check your answers and see what color repeats the most. Then, read about your personality.

 Outgoing	You are outgoing and you like to be with your friends and family. You are funny and you love to make other people laugh. However, it's hard for you to pay attention, especially if you don't find something interesting. Try to calm down and concentrate.
 Fair	You are sensitive and like helping others. You are tolerant of other people's opinions and feelings. You want everything to be fair and equal, so you treat others fairly. Try to think more about how you feel and why.
 Curious	You are very active, curious, and full of energy. You are a natural leader, and you feel proud of yourself. You like to try new things. You don't want your parents to tell you what to do. You make your own choices. Try to listen to your parents and teachers, too.
 **Responsible**	You are responsible, well-organized, and calm. You prefer to work by yourself. You don't need to be the leader. You are cautious and reserved. Try to talk and work more with your classmates.

Key Words

1 **Read and write the Key Words.**

a Do you want chocolate or vanilla ice cream? It's a hard __ __ __ __ __ __.

b My best friend is __ __ __ __ __ __ __ __. She isn't shy. She smiles at everyone and makes friends easily.

c My friend is very __ __ __ __ __ __ __ __. He accepts my opinions even when we disagree.

d I am __ __ __ __ __ __ __ __. I wear my helmet every time I ride my bike.

Comprehension

2 **Read and circle Y (Yes) or N (No).**

a In the personality test, purple represents a personality that is fair.   Y   N

b Outgoing personalities love making others laugh.   Y   N

c Curious personalities are full of energy.   Y   N

d Responsible personalities are very disorganized.   Y   N

3 **Circle the correct option to complete each sentence.**

1 Outgoing personalities have a hard time …

   a sharing their ideas.   b concentrating.   c being fair.

2 Fair personalities also need to think about …

   a their own feelings.   b their family.   c their friends.

3 Curious personalities need to listen to …

   a others.   b music.   c themselves.

4 Responsible personalities need to try to …

   a have fun.   b work more with others.   c be cautious.

Digging Deeper

4 Label the personalities according to the color test on pages 11–13. Then, match the personalities with the situations.

> fair and tolerant   curious and full of energy
> responsible and cautious   outgoing and funny

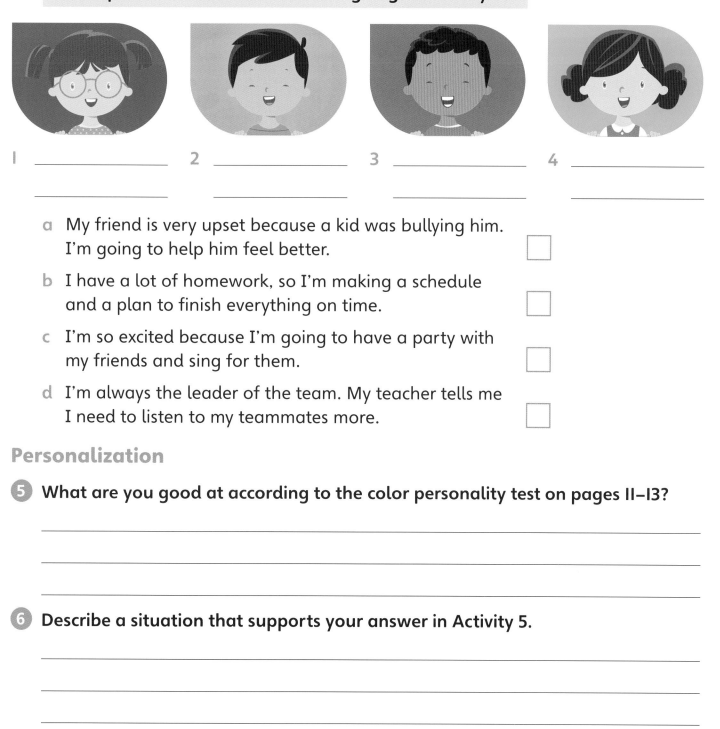

1 _____   2 _____   3 _____   4 _____

_____   _____   _____   _____

a   My friend is very upset because a kid was bullying him. I'm going to help him feel better. ☐

b   I have a lot of homework, so I'm making a schedule and a plan to finish everything on time. ☐

c   I'm so excited because I'm going to have a party with my friends and sing for them. ☐

d   I'm always the leader of the team. My teacher tells me I need to listen to my teammates more. ☐

Personalization

5 What are you good at according to the color personality test on pages 11–13?

_____

_____

_____

6 Describe a situation that supports your answer in Activity 5.

_____

_____

_____

2 What can space exploration teach us?

Key Words

1 🎧 **Preview the Key Words.**
2.1

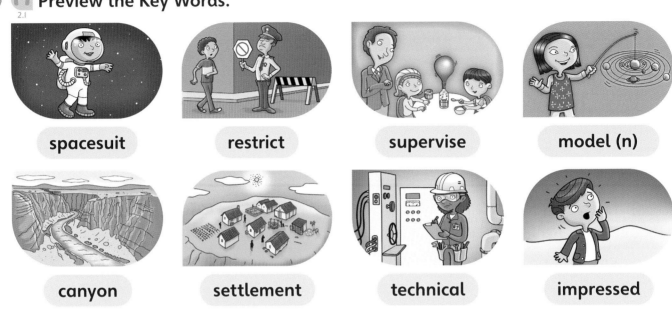

spacesuit   restrict   supervise   model (n)

canyon   settlement   technical   impressed

2 **Read the definitions and write the Key Words.**

a   feeling or showing admiration or respect for someone or
something _____

b   a place where people have come to live, where no other people lived
before _____

c   a small copy or example of something _____

d   to stop or prevent a person or a thing from doing
something _____

Pre-reading

3 👁 **Look at the pictures on pages 17–19. Circle the phrases that relate to the story.**

the moon   living on Mars   a girl's dream

plants and animals   giving a speech   robots

4 🎧 **Listen and read.**
2.2

Mars-to-Natalie

By Kellie Dundon • Illustrated by Gabriela Granados

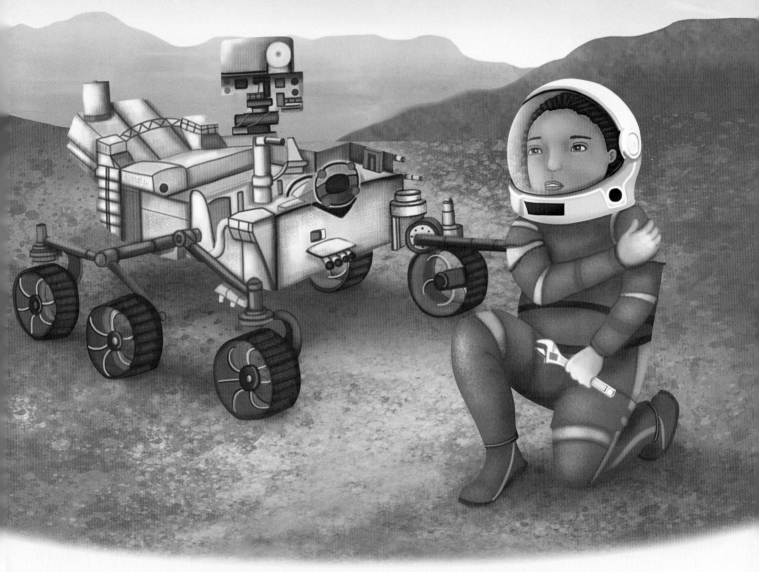

Wow, is it cold! The glow of the red light on my face is not warm at all. Life on Mars is cold—even colder than I'd imagined. Being this cold means that even small jobs are hard work. While my spacesuit keeps me safe out here, it also restricts my movements.

But I don't mind the challenges of living on Mars. I'm the first member of my family to live here. Well, the first U.S. citizen in fact!

You're probably wondering why I live on Mars, so let me explain. It's one of those crazy stories.

My story begins one day at school, when the Mars Colony 1.0 team visited. I was only ten years old. The day started like any other school day. I walked over to the auditorium to find Ms. Thomas, the science teacher. She was supervising our school project, getting it ready for our special visitors. There were models of solar systems hanging from the roof. There were posters with drawings of space missions and the planets on the walls.

Ms. Thomas noticed me watching her. She gave me a big, excited smile and waved me over.

"Great to see you, Natalie! Is your speech ready?" I nodded yes. I'd been practicing my speech about Mars for three weeks. Space was my passion. In fact, it was my obsession. Ms. Thomas knew it, which is why I'd been invited to open the special event with a presentation about the planet Mars.

Everyone knows that Mars is cold and it's far from the Sun. But almost nobody knows that Mars is red because of rusty iron in the ground or that it has dead volcanoes. Mars is half the size of Earth, has signs of ancient floods, and has canyons and polar ice caps. Sorry if I'm boring you, but I did warn you that I have an obsession with Mars!

When I still lived back on Earth, I spent most afternoons watching videos about space. My favorite ones were about the plans for Mars Colony 1.0. They were planning to set up a human settlement on Mars. To be part of the team for the first settlement, you had to be a technical and social genius. They wanted people who could build and fix things. They had to be able to invent things under pressure, too. Finally, they had to be good at getting along with others. If you have a big argument with someone on Mars, you can't just take the bus home!

I practiced my speech one last time. I was ready. I stood up in front of the whole school and told them everything I knew about Mars. It was a lot of information! The special guests looked impressed. Afterward, they wanted to talk to me.

"There's something we'd like to ask you," they said. I held my breath, hoping this was the moment I'd been waiting for.

"We were impressed by your knowledge of Mars. We'd like to invite you to join the colony, once you're old enough. If it's OK with your parents." I agreed instantly. But I had no idea how to tell Mom and Dad. They were going to miss me a lot!

"Natalie! Wake up, you'll be late for school!"

I open my eyes. That's when I realize the red light is coming from the morning sun shining through my window. So I'm not an astronaut on Mars after all. I just slept late!

But today is the day the Mars 1.0 Colony team comes to school. I get dressed quickly. I grab my speech, kiss my mom goodbye and run outside to catch my bus. There's still time to make my dream a reality!

Key Words

1 **Unscramble the Key Words and complete the sentences.**

| p-a-e-s-c-t-u-s-i | e-s-p-v-s-u-i-e-r | n-y-c-n-a-o | c-h-e-t-c-n-i-l-a |

a You have to wear a _____ when you leave the space station.

b Astronauts need _____ skills to use special equipment.

c My gym teacher likes to _____ us on the climbing ropes.

d There is a river at the bottom of the _____.

Comprehension

2 **Read and circle _T_ (true) or _F_ (false).**

a A spacesuit makes working on Mars easy.   T   F

b Natalie doesn't know anything about Mars.   T   F

c Natalie wants to join Mars Colony 1.0.   T   F

d Natalie wants to live on Mars in the future.   T   F

3 **Mark (✔) three things Natalie does in her dream.**

a Natalie does some jobs on Mars.   ☐

b She gives a speech.   ☐

c She talks to the Mars Colony 1.0 team.   ☐

d She asks her parents if she can go to live on Mars. ☐

4 **Complete the graphic organizer.**

> **The Mars Colony 1.0 team is coming to school.**
> Natalie is the first U.S. citizen on Mars.   Mars has canyons and ice caps.
> Natalie sleeps in.   The Mars team is impressed with Natalie.
> Natalie wears a spacesuit.

Dream	**Reality**
_____	The Mars Colony 1.0 team is coming to school.
_____	_____
_____	_____

5 **Look at Activity 3 on page 16. Do any of your answers change?**

Digging Deeper

6 Complete the Venn diagram. Then, add another idea to each section.

| Earth | Both | Mars |

farther from the Sun
canyons
buses
ice caps
school
dead volcanoes
human settlement
red planet
need spacesuit

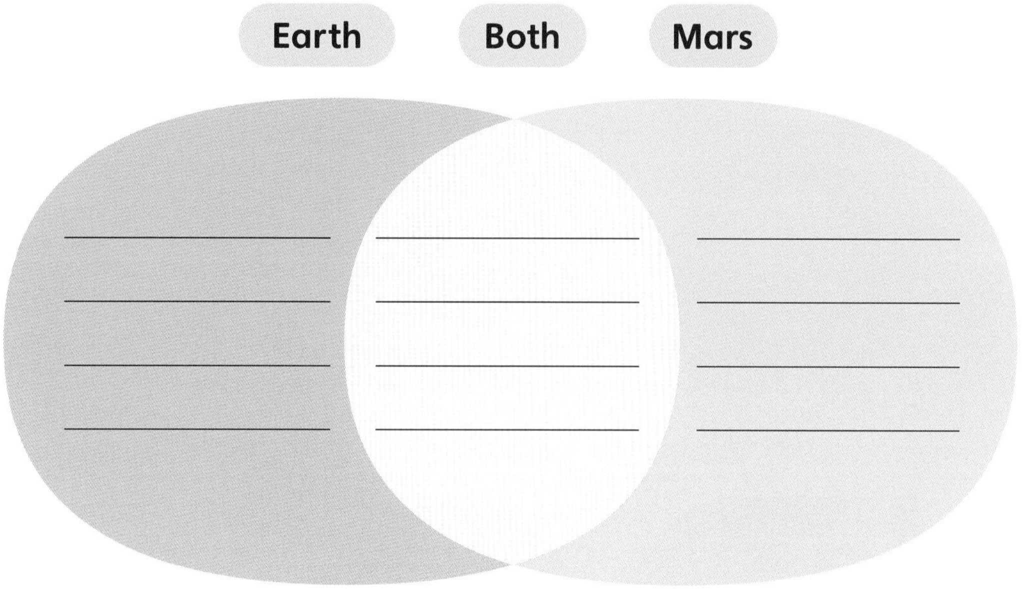

_____   _____   _____

_____   _____   _____

_____   _____   _____

_____   _____   _____

7 Circle the correct options and complete the sentences.

a In the dream, the Mars Colony 1.0 team wants / doesn't want Natalie to go to Mars because _____

_____.

b Natalie wants / doesn't want to go to Mars because _____

_____.

c There is / isn't red light shining on Natalie's face because _____

_____.

Personalization

8 Imagine you went to live on Mars. Mark (✔) three things you would take.

☐ music   ☐ art supplies   ☐ video games   ☐ a friend

☐ a pet   ☐ a soccer ball   ☐ plants   ☐ books

9 What three things would you miss the most about life on Earth? Why?

a _____

b _____

c _____

2 What can space exploration teach us?

Key Words

1 🎧 Preview the Key Words.
2.3

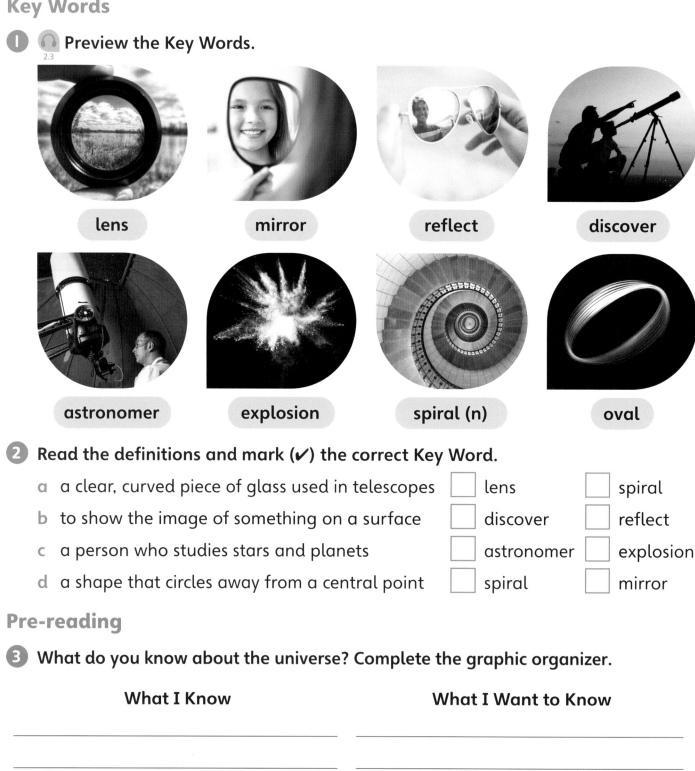

lens	mirror	reflect	discover
astronomer	explosion	spiral (n)	oval

2 Read the definitions and mark (✔) the correct Key Word.

a   a clear, curved piece of glass used in telescopes ☐ lens ☐ spiral

b   to show the image of something on a surface ☐ discover ☐ reflect

c   a person who studies stars and planets ☐ astronomer ☐ explosion

d   a shape that circles away from a central point ☐ spiral ☐ mirror

Pre-reading

3 What do you know about the universe? Complete the graphic organizer.

What I Know	What I Want to Know
_____	_____
_____	_____
_____	_____

4 🎧 Listen and read.
2.4

Exploring the Universe

By Jeremy Edgar

Galileo Galilei

Can you imagine getting into trouble for using a telescope? That's what happened to Galileo Galilei. Around 1609, people still believed that the Sun went around the Earth. Then, Galileo used a new invention and saw something different: the Earth went around the Sun! The new invention was the telescope. And people who believed that the Sun went around the Earth didn't like to be told that they were wrong. So lots of people were mad at Galileo!

Galileo found out a lot of new things about our solar system using the telescope. But there were problems with the early telescopes. One problem was the glass lenses. When light passes though glass, it sometimes breaks up into different colors. Have you seen a rainbow? That is light passing through water. It's similar when light passes through glass. So it was hard to see out of early telescopes.

Newton's Reflective Telescope

Isaac Newton solved the problem! Around 1668, instead of using a glass lens, he used a curved metal mirror to reflect light. He called his invention a reflector telescope. Reflector telescopes have two big advantages. The images are clearer. And it is easier to make the telescopes bigger—much bigger!

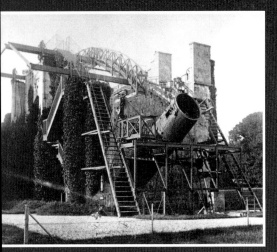

The Giant Telescope of Lord Rosse

In 1845, Lord Rosse built the world's largest telescope. It took many years to build, but it was worth it. With his awesome new telescope, Lord Rosse could see faraway nebulae and galaxies.

In the 20th century, telescopes got even bigger. But they still weren't perfect. The air in the Earth's atmosphere is always moving. This affects the light from the stars. That is why stars twinkle when we look at them.

The Hubble Space Telescope

In 1990, the Hubble Space Telescope solved that problem! When scientists look at stars from space, they don't twinkle. So the Hubble Space Telescope was placed in space, and it circles around the Earth. With the Hubble Space Telescope, scientists can see galaxies millions of light years away. (One light year is the distance that light travels in one Earth year.)

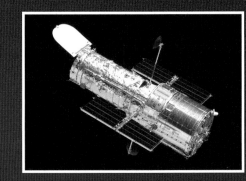

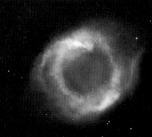

Is this nebula looking at us?

Hubble is famous for its spectacular images, like this one of a nebula. A nebula is a cloud of dust that forms after a star explodes. This one looks like an eye!

The Spitzer Space Telescope

In 2003, a new kind of space telescope was launched into space: the Spitzer Space Telescope. It used a special kind of light (infrared) that can pass through dust and clouds. It's similar to X-rays, which can pass through our bodies and give us clear images of our bones. With the information from Spitzer, scientists were able to see incredible images of stars.

TESS: Looking for Exoplanets

The Transiting Exoplanet Survey Satellite (TESS) was put into orbit in 2018. Its job is to find exoplanets. In our solar system, all planets orbit around the Sun. And exoplanets orbit around other stars. They are more difficult to find than stars because planets don't shine. TESS isn't a telescope—it's a satellite. And it has powerful cameras. TESS takes pictures of stars every two seconds, but scientists don't study every picture. They do, however, study a great number of them to see exoplanets that pass in front of the stars.

Exoplanets are hard to find.

Scientists have studied a lot of exoplanets using TESS. Many of them are gas giants like Jupiter and Saturn. Others are rocky planets like Earth. Only a few exoplanets look like they have all the things necessary for life. Scientists are very interested in learning more about them!

The JWST: An Amazing New Telescope!

The James Webb Space Telescope (JWST) will be ready in 2021. This telescope is like Hubble but even better. Scientists can't wait to use it! The new space telescope will help them answer a lot of questions. And who knows what new and wonderful things they will discover.

New Discoveries

Now you know that Galileo made some amazing discoveries with his simple telescope. With every new invention, astronomers find out more about our universe. And with every new discovery, astronomers and scientists have more questions. So, what have we learned since Galileo first pointed his telescope at the sky? Let's find out!

Jupiter and Its Moons

Galileo discovered four moons around Jupiter. But today we know there are at least 79! Astronomers can now see the original four moons more clearly. Pictures sent by Hubble show water on one of the moons. Some scientists think that there could even be life there!

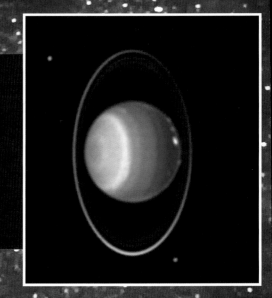

Beautiful Saturn and Its Rings

We also know a lot more about the planets in our solar system thanks to our high-tech telescopes. Saturn is made of gas, and its rings are made of ice and rocks. Astronomers have seen storms on Saturn. They look like little explosions or like popcorn popping!

Bright Clouds on Uranus

A planet that was not officially discovered until 1781 is Uranus. That is because, before then, people were not sure that what they were looking at was a planet. Uranus is very unusual. It's an ice giant made of water, gases, and other liquids. It spins on its side! It also has rings like Saturn and many moons.

The Milky Way: A Spiral Galaxy

Our solar system is part of a galaxy, which is a huge collection of gas, dust, and stars. Galaxies have different forms. We live in a spiral galaxy called the Milky Way. About 20% of the galaxies scientists can see are spiral. The Spitzer Space telescope has taken many detailed pictures of our galaxy.

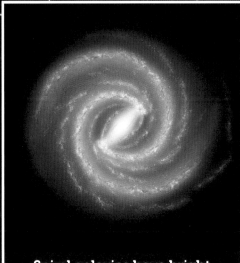

Spiral galaxies have bright, flat discs and spiral arms.

Elliptical Galaxies

Oval shaped, or elliptical, galaxies form when two or more spiral galaxies crash into each other. One day our galaxy—the Milky Way—will crash into the Andromeda Galaxy. Fortunately, that won't happen for another five billion years! This image shows a young elliptical galaxy. It is only four billion years old! About 60% of all galaxies are elliptical.

This elliptical galaxy still shows a bright disc. That's how astronomers know that it isn't very old.

A Lot of Galaxies!

So far modern telescopes have discovered 10,000 galaxies. Astronomers believe that there are over 100 billion galaxies in the universe! The smallest galaxies may have only 100,000 stars. And the biggest can contain trillions of stars. The universe is a very big place!

Key Words

1 **Read the clues. Complete the crossword puzzle with the Key Words.**

Down

1 to learn about something for the first time
2 a piece of glass that reflects images

Across

3 a sudden and noisy blast of energy and light
4 something that has the shape of an egg

Comprehension

2 **Use the names of the planets to solve the riddles.**

a You'll find ice and rocks on my rings—explosions and storms, and terrible things!

b They say I'm strange, but I have nothing to hide. I have lots of moons and spin on my side.

c Look at my moons, you can clearly see four. But look closer and you'll see even more!

_____   _____   _____

3 **Answer the questions.**

a **When** did Galileo prove the Earth went around the Sun?_____

b **What** kind of light does the Spitzer Telescope use? _____

c Which planets in the article are described as "gas giants"? _____

d **What** is the name of our galaxy?_____

4 **Complete the timeline.**

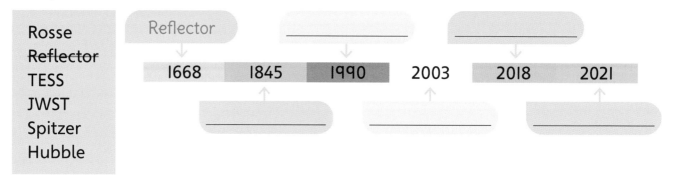

Rosse
Reflector
TESS
JWST
Spitzer
Hubble

Reflector _____ _____

1668   1845   1990   2003   2018   2021

_____   _____   _____

Digging Deeper

5 🔊 **Complete the graphic organizer.**

> Scientists use TESS to study exoplanets.

> They are a collection of gas, dust, and stars.

> Uranus spins on its side and it's an ice giant.

> There might be over 100 billion galaxies in the universe!

> The Spitzer uses infrared light to study stars.

> Elliptical galaxies form when spiral galaxies crash into each other.

> Saturn is made of gas.

> Jupiter has at least 79 moons.

> The Hubble studies galaxies millions of light years away.

Main Idea	Detail I	Detail 2	Detail 3
a Our solar system is an amazing place.			
b Modern telescopes and satellites have helped scientists.			
c Galaxies have different characteristics.			

Personalization

6 **Look at the chart you completed on page 22. Write three things you learned.**

a _____

b _____

c _____

7 **Imagine you are an astronomer. Which planet would you like to study most? Why?**

_____

_____

3 Is technology good or bad?

Key Words

1 🎧 **Preview the Key Words.**
3.1

| leftovers | nutritional | mess | promise (v) |

| eliminate | feature (n) | trial | scan (v) |

2 **Read the glossary entries and write the Key Words.**

a _____ *noun* a characteristic of something

b _____ *verb* to remove something that is not wanted or needed

c _____ *adjective* containing what keeps your body healthy

d _____ *noun* something that is in a dirty or disorderly state

Pre-reading

3 **Look at the pictures on pages 31–35 and circle the correct options.**

What is the story about?	Where does it happen?	When does it take place?
a robot that does chores	on another planet	in the past
a lazy family	in a house and a store	in the present
an accident at home	at a swimming pool	in the future

4 🎧 **Listen and read.**
3.2

Charlie the Chorebot

By Kim Milne & Illustrated by Axel Rangel

Scene 1: In the Kitchen

[In the kitchen, Mom is complaining to the twins about their unhealthy eating habits and the household chores they refuse to do.]

Mom: Here you are, guys—it's our Monday special! I used the leftovers from Sunday's dinner, cooked chicken, and added some veggies and pasta.

Dad: Looks delicious!

Taylor: [She stares at the plate.] Mom! I've decided that I'm only going to eat beige-colored foods from now on, so I'll just have the pasta and the chicken, please!

Mom: Taylor, you know about eating the rainbow, and that the neutral-colored foods usually score low in nutritional value.
[She sighs.] Tyler, pass your plate, please!

Tyler: Mom, I've decided that I don't want to eat trees anymore.

Mom: Well, I'm glad you're eco-friendly, Tyler, but they're not trees! They're broccoli.

Tyler: Well, they look like small trees to me!

Mom: Good grief. We can't make different meals for all of us every day!

Dad: So, guys … how's your chore chart going?

Tyler: Dad, I promise Taylor said she was going to clean the rooms this time, and I would do it next time.

Taylor: I did! I know they look messy, but I already cleaned them. I just made a mess again.

Mom: Stop it, please! Could one of you unload the dishwasher and the other clear the table once you finish eating your food? And when you've done that, the garbage needs to be taken out and the pool needs cleaning.

Tyler:	Sorry, Mom. I was coughing all night, and I have a horrible headache. I probably have an allergy from pulling weeds yesterday. Can't somebody else do it?
Taylor:	No … I have to make a vinegar and baking soda car for my science class.
Mom:	[SHE SHAKES HER HEAD.] You know, I've had enough of this!
Dad:	Me, too. But I have an idea. Let's go to BotCom, the company that sells ChoreBots.
Mom:	Let's do it!

Scene 2: At the Store

[THE FAMILY LISTENS CAREFULLY TO THE ROBOT SALESMAN.]

Salesman:	This is the newest model from our collection of ChoreBots. In fact, you'll be its first owner. I promise it'll make your daily life so much easier!
Mom:	Well, it looks cute, but what can it do?
Salesman:	It eliminates those repetitive and boring tasks you all have to do every day!

[TAYLOR AND TYLER GIVE EACH OTHER A HIGH FIVE AND CHEER.]

Dad:	You mean like cutting the grass and taking out the garbage?
Salesman:	Exactly!
Mom:	What about cooking and doing the laundry?
Salesman:	The ChoreBot can do it all! Before, you needed a whole army of robots to do the household chores. Now, they're all integrated into one.
Tyler:	Does it clean rooms?
Salesman:	Yes. It dusts, mops, and vacuums, as well as picks up and puts away clothes!
Tyler:	Mom, Dad—we have to get one of these!
Taylor:	Please!
Dad:	Well, it does seem to be the solution to our problems.
Mom:	Yes, but is it safe? I've read some bad reviews!

Salesman:	Yes, it's totally reliable, and it has an added feature. It can learn from its environment and its experiences. That means it can build on its skills based on that knowledge. So it can learn new things all by itself!
Mom:	Oh ... I'm not sure. What about working together as a team and sharing responsibilities?
Taylor:	Yes, but think of all the extra time we'll have to study, Mom!
Tyler:	And play video games!
Mom:	I'm not sure!
Salesman:	Well ... [He unveils the model.] We have this particular model. You can have a free day's trial!
Mom:	[She looks at it carefully.] OK then!

[CC switches itself on, opens its eyes, and scans the room. It speaks to the family.]

CC:	Good afternoon. Pleased to meet you. I'm Charlie the ChoreBot, but you can call me CC.

Scene 3: Breakfast Time!

[In the kitchen, CC waits patiently for everyone. Mom enters first.]

CC:	Good morning. What would you like for breakfast? We have vegetarian egg-filled tacos, Japanese cabbage pancakes, or spicy potato waffles with a variety of beverages.
Mom:	Coffee and waffles would be great, thanks.

[Dad enters the kitchen, whistling.]

CC:	Good morning. [CC instantly starts imitating the song.] What would you like today, vegetarian egg-filled tacos, Japanese cabbage pancakes, or spicy potato waffles?
Dad:	[Dad gets annoyed.] I was just whistling that tune. Um ... I'll try the pancakes with a coconut mocha iced coffee, please!

Mom: Wow, these are the most delicious waffles I've ever eaten!

[TAYLOR ENTERS THE KITCHEN COMPLETELY SURPRISED.]

Taylor: You won't believe it. When I woke up, the room was really neat and clean. Everything had been put away during the night, so I couldn't find anything!

[TYLER ENTERS THE KITCHEN COMPLETELY HAPPY.]

Tyler: Wow! My room is so neat that I was able to play a complete video game before breakfast!

Dad: Have you done your math homework?

Tyler: Yes, CC did it in five seconds. It would have taken me at least 20 minutes if I'd done it!

Mom: Really, Tyler? You're supposed to do your homework yourself! Now, come here please, CC! I've written a list of all your chores for today.
I'd like you to mow the backyard, throw out the garbage, do the laundry, mop and dust all the rooms, and … um … clean the swimming pool and make us a nice hot meal for dinner!

CC: Affirmative!

Taylor: You do all that in one day and go to work, too?

Parents: Yes!

Scene 4: Wrecked Home!

[IN THE KITCHEN, CC IS COOKING WHEN THE FAMILY ENTERS CHATTING AND LAUGHING.]

Mom: Mmm! Smells delicious, like Asian spices. Did you get all the chores done, too?

CC: Affirmative!

[CC AUTOMATICALLY IMITATES DAD'S FAVORITE MUSIC LOUDLY.]

Dad: [HE STARTS YELLING.] No, not now CC. Have you seen the backyard? All my beautiful Dutch tulip heads have been chopped off, and the garbage has been scattered all over the backyard!

Taylor: [SHE STARTS SCREAMING.] Quickly, call the police, we've been robbed. The thieves emptied out all my drawers and threw everything on the floor.

Tyler: Look outside! The pool's like a gigantic bubble bath.

[EVERYONE LOOKS AT CC WHO IS CALMLY COOKING.]

Mom: What have you done, CC?

CC: Everything you asked me to do. I threw out the garbage, mowed the backyard, cleaned the pool, and I put all Taylor and Tyler's clothes on the floor so that they could find them easily! They said they couldn't find them when I picked them up and put them away.

Mom: Oh, CC! Well … at least dinner is ready.

CC: Affirmative!

[CC STARTS SERVING THE FOOD.]

Taylor: Yuck! It's disgusting! It's all gooey like snail slime.

Tyler: Phew! It's really spicy, too!

[TAYLOR AND TYLER DRINK A LOT OF WATER AND FAN THEIR MOUTHS.]

CC: But you told me to make a HOT dinner.

Mom: Yes … but I meant temperature hot, not spicy hot!

Scene 5: No More CC!

[THE NEXT DAY EVERYONE IS BEING VERY COOPERATIVE.]

Dad: Would anyone like more pasta?

Mom: Oh, yes, please!

Taylor: Me, too … By the way, Mom, you were right—beige food is low in nutritional value, so I'm only eating red and white food from now on! Like rice! Oh, and I folded the laundry.

Mom: [SHE'S SURPRISED.] Really? Great!

Tyler: And I cleaned our rooms.

Mom: Wonderful!

Dad: And I took CC back to BotCom! What a disaster!

[EVERYONE LAUGHS. NEXT, THEY ARE SITTING AT THE TABLE, EATING DINNER, AND LOOKING VERY HAPPY.]

Key Words

1 Read and complete the text with the correct Key Words.

We are trying out the robot for a free (1)_____. The robot has special vision. For example, it (2)_____ the floor quickly, looking for any mess and then cleans the room. It also collects the food we didn't eat at lunch. It uses those (3)_____ from lunch to make soup for dinner. The robot store (4)_____ to give us a special price if we decide to keep the robot.

Comprehension

2 Match the sentence halves.

1	CC the robot whistles Dad's tune, and Dad …	a	plays a video game.
2	It cleans Taylor's room, so she …	b	gets annoyed.
3	It does Tyler's homework, so he …	c	nobody likes.
4	It makes a hot, spicy dinner that …	d	can't find anything.

3 Number the events in order.

a The next day, CC does a bad job with everything. ☐

b Dad has an idea to go to BotCom. ☐

c The salesman offers the family a day's free trial with the ChoreBot. ☐

d Dad takes CC back to the store. ☐

e The twins don't want to eat healthy food or do chores. ☐

f At first, CC makes a delicious breakfast, and everyone is happy. ☐

4 Find eight chores on pages 31–35 and write them on the note.

a _____   e _____

b _____   f _____

c _____   g _____

d _____   h _____

5 Look at Activity 3 on page 30. Do any of your answers change?

Digging Deeper

6 📧 **Read the play on pages 31–35 again. Then, complete the graphic organizer.**

Main Idea	Details
a The twins do not want to do chores or eat the food that Mom makes.	Food: _____ _____ Chores: _____ _____
b CC cooks food and does chores around the house.	Food: _____ _____ Chores: _____ _____
c Life at home changes after Dad takes CC back to BotCom.	Food: _____ _____ Chores: _____ _____

Personalization

7 **Imagine you have your own robot. Write three things you would like it to do.**

_____

_____

8 **Imagine you work at BotCom. Draw your robot and write an ad.**

The (name of robot) _____

can _____

_____

_____

_____

_____

3 Is technology good or bad?

Key Words

1 🎧 **Preview the Key Words.**
3.3

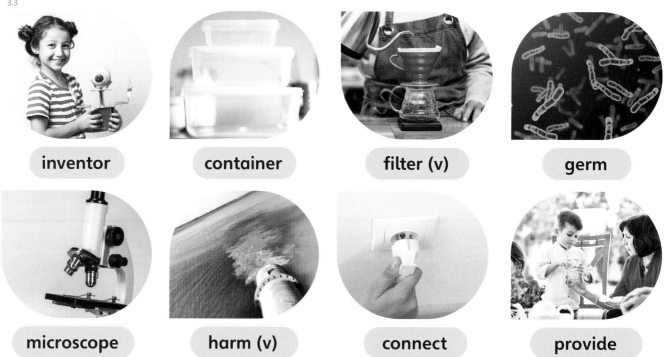

inventor   container   filter (v)   germ

microscope   harm (v)   connect   provide

2 **Read and write the Key Words.**

a We ___ ___ ___ ___ ___ ___ water to make sure it is safe to drink.

b Burning oil and gas will ___ ___ ___ ___ the environment.

c These lakes ___ ___ ___ ___ ___ ___ ___ the city with fresh water.

d The scientist looked at the bacteria under the ___ ___ ___ ___ ___ ___ ___ ___ ___ ___.

Pre-reading

3 **Look at the pictures on pages 39–41. Read the statements and mark (✔).**

The article is about ...	Yes, I agree.	No, I disagree.	I don't know.
a animals.			
b new inventions.			
c old inventions.			

4 🎧 **Listen and read.**
3.4

Low Technology— High Impact!

By Robert Gareth Vaughan

Have you ever heard of Alexander Graham Bell, Thomas Edison, or Tim Berners-Lee? They are all inventors. Without Bell and Edison, we might not have telephones or light bulbs! And thanks to Berners-Lee, we have the World Wide Web and the Internet.

These high-tech inventions are amazing; they changed our world. But simple inventions can change the world, too. And sometimes they are better for our planet!

Water Collecting Made Easy

Millions of women walk many kilometers every day to get water for their families. But an invention called the Hippo Roller is helping them! The Hippo Roller is a strong plastic container with a handle. You can push it along the ground. It's fast and easy!

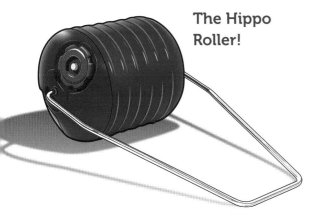

The Hippo Roller!

The Straw That Saves Lives

Sometimes water isn't clean. Don't worry! A simple invention called the LifeStraw can help. It works like a normal drinking straw, but it filters the water so that germs don't go into your mouth! This prevents dangerous diseases, like cholera.

The Foldscope

We also stop diseases with microscopes. We use them to identify things that cause disease. But microscopes are expensive and hard to carry. So Manu Prakash invented the paper microscope. It has all the same parts as a normal microscope, but it's made from a sheet of paper! And this *origami* microscope called Foldscope is not expensive!

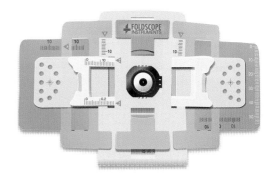

Cooking with Sunlight

People all over the world cook with wood. But this harms our environment. Every year, 18.7 million acres of forest is cut down. This is the size of 20 million football fields! The smoke from burning wood can also damage health. Fortunately, there are now safer stoves, like the solar stove. This uses energy from the sun to cook food or to kill germs in milk.

Approximately three billion people use open fires to cook.

The temperature range for this solar stove can be 66°C–204°C!

Xóchitl Cruz López: A Young Inventor!

One of Mexico's most famous young inventors is Xóchitl Cruz. She is only eight years old! Recently, Xóchitl won a prize for a solar-powered water heater. She made her heater from recycled materials, like plastic bottles and hoses. Xóchitl is from Chiapas, which is a poor state in southern Mexico. Her invention can help people in Chiapas have hot water. It also means that people use fewer trees for wood to heat water for cooking.

Xóchitl's water heater is similar to this one!

Soccer = Electricity!

What if a soccer ball made energy when you kicked it? Well, that's what the Soccket Ball does! When you use the ball for 30 minutes, you get three hours of electricity. You can even connect a lamp directly to the ball! This means kids can read or study when it gets dark. The Soccket Ball, invented by Jessica O. Matthews and her team, makes a huge difference in places that don't have access to electricity.

About a billion people in the world don't have electricity.

William Kamkwamba: A Young Innovator!

William grew up in a small village in Malawi that didn't have electricity. William wanted to study, but he had to leave school because his family couldn't pay for it. One day, he remembered a picture of a windmill in a textbook from school. What did he do? He decided to make his own windmill with old car and bicycle parts. He then had a better idea. He would provide electricity for the whole village! At first, some people in his village thought the windmill was a silly idea. But pretty soon they were charging their cell phones with electricity from William's windmill! William is an adult now and is working on projects to help others all around the world.

Malawi is one of the most beautiful, but poorest, countries in Africa.

Start Inventing!

These are just a few of the inventions that are helping both people and the environment. Inventions don't need to be high-tech to make a difference. They don't have to be something new either!

All it takes is one great idea!

Can you think of an idea or invention to change the world? What are you waiting for?

Key Words

1 **Find the Key Words. Then, complete the definitions.**

S	A	Z	C	D	I	F	G	C
T	R	O	O	U	R	W	S	O
E	D	C	N	R	A	I	G	N
F	F	B	N	N	L	J	E	T
I	N	V	E	N	T	O	R	A
L	A	D	C	H	O	K	M	I
T	V	W	T	A	F	G	N	N
E	I	P	R	O	V	I	D	E
R	Q	S	A	F	G	H	B	R

a to join two things together _____

b an object, such as a box, that can hold something _____

c a very small living thing that causes disease _____

d to pass a liquid through something that removes things you don't want _____

e someone who makes something for the first time _____

f to give something that is wanted or needed _____

Comprehension

2 **Use the names of the inventions to solve the riddles.**

a Have a drink with me, you know you should. I filtered out the germs. The water tastes good!

b You use me to see things that are very small. You can see germs and bugs, and that's not all.

c Kick me around, and I'll give you light. This means you can study at night!

_____   _____   _____

3 **Circle the correct option to complete each sentence.**

1 The Hippo Roller helps people …

a cook.   b heat water.   c carry water.

2 The Foldscope was invented by …

a Xóchitl Cruz.   b Manu Prakash.   c Jessica Matthews.

3 Soccket Balls and windmills help provide …

a electricity.   b water.   c heat.

4 **Look at Activity 3 on page 38. Do any of your answers change?**

Digging Deeper

5 🖱 **Read and circle _M_ (main idea) or _D_ (detail).**

		M	D
a	The Hippo Roller makes carrying water fast and easy.	M	D
b	The Foldscope is made of paper.	M	D
c	The Soccket Ball is a soccer ball that generates electricity.	M	D
d	The Foldscope is a portable, inexpensive microscope.	M	D
e	The Soccket Ball can give you three hours of electricity.	M	D
f	The Hippo Roller is a strong plastic container with a handle.	M	D

6 🖱 **Match the main ideas with the details.**

1 The LifeStraw is a simple invention that cleans water. ☐

2 William Kamkwamba is an inventor from Malawi. ☐

3 The solar stove uses energy from the sun. ☐

4 Xóchitl Cruz López is one of Mexico's youngest inventors. ☐

a He built a windmill with old parts to provide electricity to his village.

b She invented a solar-powered heater from recycled materials.

c It filters water so that germs don't go into your mouth.

d It can get as hot as 204°C!

Personalization

7 **Imagine you are asked to invent something to help your community.**

a Mark (✔) or write your own idea.   b Draw your invention. What is it called?

☐ water pollution

☐ air pollution

☐ traffic

☐ garbage on streets

☐ noise pollution

☐ _____

 How do we entertain ourselves?

Key Words

1 🎧 **Preview the Key Words.**
4.1

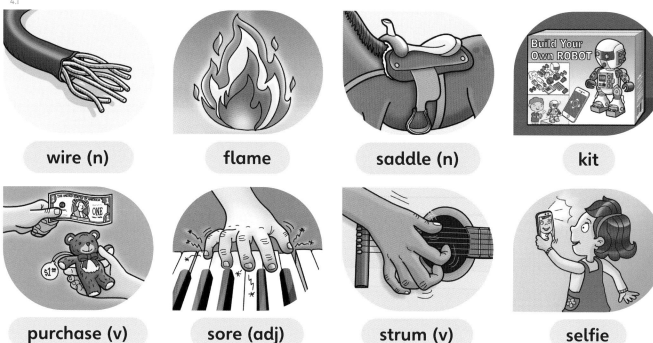

wire (n)	flame	saddle (n)	kit
purchase (v)	sore (adj)	strum (v)	selfie

2 **Match the definitions with the Key Words.**

1	a photo you take of yourself	a sore
2	when something hurts or is uncomfortable	b kit
3	a part of fire or something burning	c selfie
4	a set of parts or tools to make something	d flame

Pre-reading

3 **Look at the pictures on pages 45–47. Circle *Yes* or *No*.**

a	The poems are about animals and plants.	Yes No
b	The poems are about doing fun things.	Yes No
c	There are robots, musical instruments, and sports.	Yes No
d	The poems are about having fun with friends at a park.	Yes No

4 🎧 **Listen and read.**
4.2

We're Going to Learn to Build Robots

By Kenn Nesbitt · Illustrated by Sheila Cabeza de Vaca

We're going to learn to build robots at school.
I'm going to make mine look totally cool.
I'll build it with switches and light bulbs and wires,
Computers, TVs, and bulldozer tires.

We're going to learn to build robots at school.
The light from the sun will give mine all its fuel.
I plan to create one that's fifty feet tall.
I'll make it so strong it can break down a wall.

We're going to learn to build robots at school.
And mine will be able to conquer and rule.
I'll paint it with lightning and flames on the sides
And give it a saddle to take it for rides.

We're going to learn to build robots at school.
But now I am feeling a bit like a fool.
We're going to make them with kits from the mall.
The robots we're building are three inches tall.

If You Buy Me a Piano

By Kenn Nesbitt · Illustrated by Sheila Cabeza de Vaca

If you buy me a piano,
I will practice every day.
I'll become an awesome pianist.
I'll really learn to play.

If you buy me a guitar, then
I will write a song for you.
I'll become a great guitarist and
A famous rock star, too.

If you purchase me a drum set,
I will play until I'm sore.
I'll become the finest drummer
That you've ever heard before.

If my plinking and my strumming
And my "rat-a-tat-a-tat"
Are too loud, please buy a tablet,
And I'll learn to play with that.

Rules
I Must Remember

By Kenn Nesbitt · Illustrated by Sheila Cabeza de Vaca

I must not take a selfie
When I'm running in a race.
I must catch baseballs with my glove
Instead of with my face.

I have to tie my shoes before
I start a soccer match.
I do not have to do my homework
When I'm playing catch.

I must remember all these rules
If I expect to play.
I'll have to start tomorrow.
I forgot them all today.

Key Words

1 **Read and write the Key Words.**

   a Put the ___ ___ ___ ___ ___ ___ on the horse before you ride.

   b There is a loose ___ ___ ___ ___ coming out of the cable.

   c You have to ___ ___ ___ ___ ___ the strings on the guitar to make a sound.

   d We have to ___ ___ ___ ___ ___ ___ ___ ___ a gift for Mom's birthday.

Comprehension

2 **Read and write the titles of the poems on pages 45–47.**

| a | This poem is about a boy who loves music so much and will practice a lot to become the best. | b | This poem is about a girl who plays sports, but must follow instructions to play them safely. | c | This poem is about a girl who loves new technology and wants to build something very big. |

_____   _____   _____

3 **Answer the questions.**

   a Why does the girl in one of the poems feel like a fool? _____

_____

   b What musical instruments are mentioned in one of the poems? _____

_____

   c When must the girl not take a selfie? _____

4 **Find a word you don't understand on pages 45–47. Complete the chart.**

   a Write the word.

   _____

   b Is it a noun, verb, adjective, or adverb?

   _____

   c Look for clues in the pictures and the sentence before and after. What do you think the word means?

   _____

   d Ask your teacher or look it up in the dictionary. Write the meaning.

   _____

Digging Deeper

5 **Read and circle the rhyming pairs in the same color.**

We're going to learn to build robots at school.
The light from the sun will give mine all its fuel.
I plan to create one that's fifty feet tall.
I'll make it so strong it can break down a wall.

I have to tie my shoes before
I start a soccer match.
I do not have to do my homework
When I'm playing catch.

6 **Read and mark (✔) what makes words rhyme.**

☐ Words rhyme because they are at the end of a sentence.

☐ Words rhyme because they are close together.

☐ Words rhyme because they have similar ending sounds.

7 **Circle the words that rhyme in the same color. Complete the verse.**

questions

car

lessons

star

I want to be a piano (1) _____

And drive a brand new (2) _____.

I asked my mom about it.

She said I must take (3) _____,

Instead of asking so many (4) _____.

Personalization

8 **Which poem did you like the most? Why?**

_____

_____

_____

9 **Do you like to write poetry? Why or why not?**

_____

_____

_____

4 How do we entertain ourselves?

Key Words

1 🎧 Preview the Key Words.
4.3

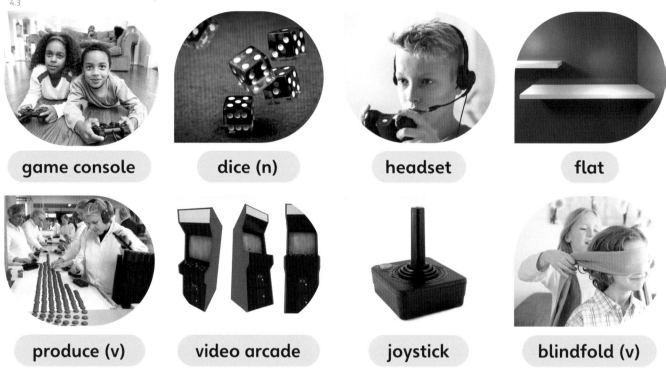

game console   dice (n)   headset   flat

produce (v)   video arcade   joystick   blindfold (v)

2 Read the glossary entries and write the Key Words.

a _____ *noun* a place where you can pay to play video games

b _____ *verb* to cover the eyes with something, like a cloth

c _____ *noun* a piece of electronic equipment to play video games

d _____ *adjective* having a smooth surface

Pre-reading

3 Look at the pictures on pages 51–57. Circle the phrases that relate to the article.

walking to school   playing games in ancient times

playing video games   protecting animals

helping the environment   playing board games

4 🎧 Listen and read.
4.4

Let's Play

By Steph Kilen

The Gaming Game

Trivia games test how well players know different facts.
Here's your chance to test your gaming knowledge!

1 Until the 19th century, who played most board games?
   a children
   b rich people, kings, and queens
   c farmers

2 What famous building will be helped by video game graphics?
   a the Taj Mahal in India
   b the Colosseum in Rome
   c the Notre Dame Cathedral in Paris

3 What was found in King Tut's tomb?
   a a board game
   b a game console
   c playing cards

4 Where was the oldest known game found?
   a Russia
   b an unnamed island in the Atlantic Ocean
   c Turkey

5 What video game characters were famous in the 1980s?
   a Donkey Kong and PAC-MAN
   b Mickey Mouse and Donald Duck
   c Ratchet and Clank

6 What was special about the 2017 world record for 48,400 points in level 1 of Angry Birds?
   a The girl who won it was three years old.
   b The boy who won it was blindfolded.
   c The winner was a dog.

7 What were the original dice made of?
   a bones
   b wood
   c cheese

8 One of the first home video games was like table tennis. What was it called?
   a Hit it!
   b Tennis Hit
   c Pong

9 What equipment do people use to play virtual reality games?
   a a headset
   b a floor mat
   c a time machine

10 How old is the oldest known game?
   a 300 years old
   b 5,000 years old
   c 25,000 years old

Check your score.

1 b	2 c	3 a	4 c	5 a	6 b	7 a	8 c	9 a	10 b

1–3 correct: Looks like you need to play again.

4–6 correct: Well played! But you should try some new games.

7–9 correct: You really know how to have fun!

10 correct: You are a gaming expert!

What About You?

What was the first game you ever played? Was it cards? A board game? Maybe a video game? What games do you play with your family? Or with your friends?

Did you know?

Everyone you know has probably played a game at some time. In fact, people around the world have enjoyed games for thousands of years!

For Thousands of Years?!

People who lived in ancient times liked to have fun, too. The oldest known game is 5,000 years old. It's a set of 49 painted stones found in Turkey. Similar games have been found in the Middle East, Europe, and Northwest Africa. Many games were "roll-and-move" games. In these games, the players rolled something to decide how far they could move their game piece. Each player wanted to be the first one to reach the finish line.

Even King Tut of Ancient Egypt played board games. A board game was found in his tomb!

Ancient board game located in Croatia.

Roll Those Bones

We are all familiar with dice—the six-sided cubes with a different number on each side. But what did people use before they had the tools or time to make them? The ankle bones of animals, often sheep or oxen! These bones have two round sides that can't be landed on. They also have four flat sides. These sides decided the player's move. Later, the ancient Mesopotamians made dice with six sides.

Who Says Only Kings Can Have Fun?

While games have been played for thousands of years, fancier board games were mostly for rich and royal people, while working people played card and dice games. But in the mid-19th century, more people had more free time. The United States started to produce a lot of board games. This made them less expensive and easier to buy. Soon, in addition to cards, many houses had board games, too. Since then, board games have become more and more popular. Many traditional games, such as checkers, Scrabble, and Monopoly, are still played by a lot of people. And every year, there are new board games. Some are based on current movies, cartoon characters, or TV shows.

Screen Time!

Like nearly everything else in our lives, games have also made their way to the computer. The first video games became popular in the late 1970s and early 1980s. The really cool ones were as big as a refrigerator! Donkey Kong and PAC-MAN were super popular. The characters were famous. The graphics were colorful, but simple by today's standards. People had to go to special places called video arcades to play. And they had to put a coin into the machine to start playing.

The Beginning of Home Video Games

There were video games played at home that connected to the TV. These games were expensive and weren't as fun as the games in the video arcades. The graphics were just pixelated green lines on black screens. One of the first home games was called Pong. It was like table tennis. Two lines on either side represented the players. A dot that represented the ball, moved *very* slowly across the screen. You used a joystick to move your piece and pushed a button to hit the ball. Boring, right? But in the 1980s, Pong was very exciting. Most people in the 80s didn't have personal computers or cell phones yet!

World Records

All games feature some form of competition. But what would it mean to play a game better than *anyone*?

- In 2015, a 10-year-old boy in England survived a million-meter fall into a solid block in the video game Minecraft.
- Two players in the United States finished a game of checkers in 20.98 seconds in 2015.
- In 2017, a Swedish boy earned 48,400 points on Level 1 of the video game Angry Birds while he was blindfolded!
- The record for most games of chess played by one person at the same time was set in 2011 by an Iranian man. He played 135 games at once.

Welcome to the 21st Century!

In today's video games, not only can you play sports as your favorite player, but you can also build worlds and create stories! And the graphics look more like movies than blinking lights. How realistic are the graphics? The Notre-Dame Cathedral in Paris, France, appears in one popular game. Much of the cathedral was destroyed by fire in 2019. The graphics in the game were designed so accurately and have so much detail, they may be used to guide people in rebuilding the cathedral.

Virtual Reality

Have you ever wished you could live inside a video game? Can you imagine changing the view of the game just by moving your head? What if instead of pressing a button on a controller to pick up something in the game, you could just use your own hand? The newest games use virtual reality. Special headsets make players feel like they are actually inside the game. It won't be long until virtual reality game sets are as popular as the consoles we use now.

Luckily, most homes have a board game *and* a computer of some form. Play a board game with your family. Spend an afternoon with a friend playing video games. Or make a long car, train, or plane trip less boring by playing your favorite game on a smartphone. Now you know how games are connected to the ancient past *and* the future.

57

Key Words

1 Find the Key Words. Then, complete the sentences.

W	X	T	L	N	J	Q	W
F	S	W	L	J	O	H	F
R	C	Q	Q	N	Y	Y	R
D	H	E	A	D	S	E	T
K	X	C	K	B	T	C	C
L	I	Q	B	D	I	C	E
P	R	O	D	U	C	E	R
K	E	W	C	T	K	Q	D

a I wear my _____ when I talk to my friend online.

b My friends and I use _____ when we play board games.

c Mom told me that she used a _____ to play PAC-MAN when she was young.

d Korea and Japan _____ lots of video games.

Comprehension

2 Read and circle *Yes* or *No*.

a The oldest board game ever found is 500 years old.   Yes   No

b King Tut probably played board games.   Yes   No

c PAC-MAN was a famous board game in the 1980s.   Yes   No

d Virtual reality games need a special headset.   Yes   No

3 Circle the correct option to complete each sentence.

1 Many of the ancient games were ...

   a so much fun.   b made of gold.   c "roll-and-move."

2 In ancient times, people didn't have dice, so they used ...

   a animal bones.   b marbles.   c wood.

3 The earliest video game, Pong, was like ...

   a PAC-MAN.   b table tennis.   c a board game.

4 Modern video games have ...

   a green lights.   b a joystick.   c realistic graphics.

5 In the past, rich and royal people mostly played with ...

   a dice.   b board games.   c cards.

6 Most people in the 1980s didn't have a ...

   a TV.   b computer.   c telephone.

Digging Deeper

4 🔊 **Read the article sections and answer the questions about inferences. Mark (✔).**

The ankle bones of animals were used in board games in ancient times. These bones had two round sides and four flat sides.	1 **Why did they use those bones?** a to eat them after the game ☐ b to know how many spaces to move ☐
While games have been played for thousands of years, fancier board games were mostly for rich and royal people.	2 **Why were they mostly for wealthy people?** a Because they were expensive. ☐ b Because wealthy people didn't have free time. ☐
In today's video games, not only can you play sports as your favorite player, but you can also build worlds and create stories! The graphics look more realistic than the old blinking lights.	3 **Why are the graphics more realistic?** a Because technology has evolved. ☐ b Because they have more colors. ☐
The newest games use virtual reality with special headsets. It won't be long until virtual reality game sets are as popular as the consoles we use now.	4 **Why will headsets be as popular as the consoles?** a Because they will be everywhere. ☐ b Because they won't be as expensive. ☐

Personalization

5 **What is your favorite board game or video game? Why is it your favorite?**

_____

_____

_____

6 **What is the most popular board game or video game in your country? Why do you think it's so popular?**

_____

_____

_____

5 What can history teach us?

Key Words

1 🎧 5.1 **Preview the Key Words.**

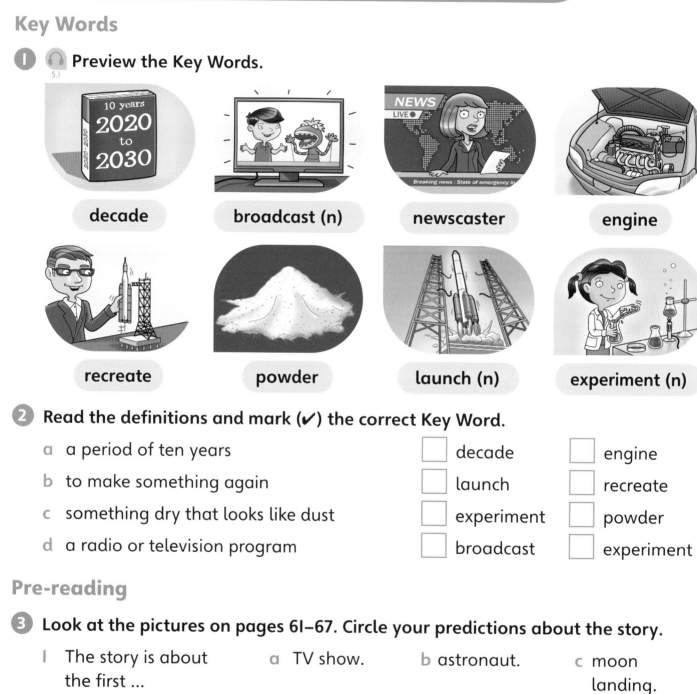

decade   broadcast (n)   newscaster   engine

recreate   powder   launch (n)   experiment (n)

2 **Read the definitions and mark (✔) the correct Key Word.**

a a period of ten years   ☐ decade   ☐ engine

b to make something again   ☐ launch   ☐ recreate

c something dry that looks like dust   ☐ experiment   ☐ powder

d a radio or television program   ☐ broadcast   ☐ experiment

Pre-reading

3 **Look at the pictures on pages 61–67. Circle your predictions about the story.**

1 The story is about the first ... a TV show. b astronaut. c moon landing.

2 The main character is ... a a young girl. b a young boy. c an astronaut.

3 The story takes place ... a on a spaceship. b on the moon. c on Earth.

4 Everything happens ... a in the past. b in the present. c in the future.

4 🎧 5.2 **Listen and read.**

One Small Step

By Steph Kilen • Illustrated by Marco Antonio Reyes

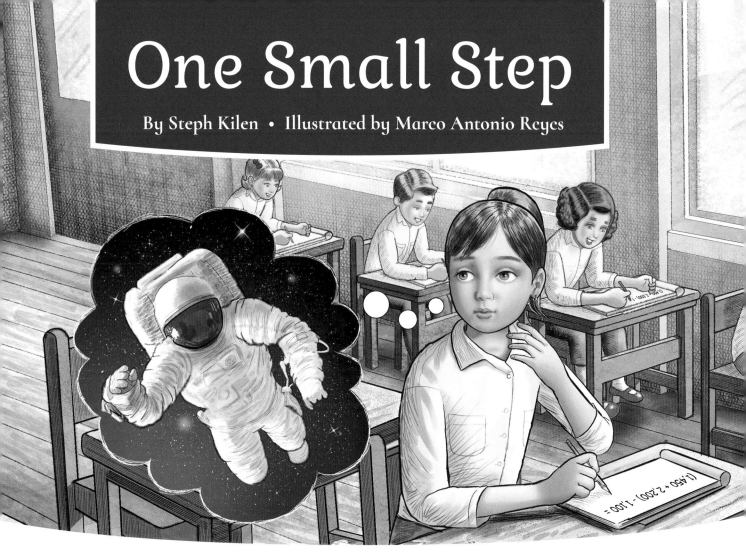

People had been talking about it all day, everywhere Sally went—at the park, at the grocery store with her mom. Her dad had told her that eight years before, President Kennedy had promised to put a man on the Moon by the end of the decade. Now, on July 20, 1969, it was finally happening! And it was going to be on TV. Some people, including her dad, got the day off work so they could watch at home. The Graysons were coming over to watch it with them. It was more exciting than a birthday party!

In math class, their teacher had told them that NASA was the big organization that explored space. They learned that a lot of people who were good at math and science worked there, not just astronauts. Math was always Sally's favorite subject. Now she liked it even more.

While they waited for the broadcast to begin, Sally's twin brother, Tommy, and Jeff Grayson wanted to play astronauts in the backyard.

"I'll be the person at NASA helping the astronauts," Sally said.

"You can't work at NASA. You're a girl!" Tommy said.

"Watch," said Jeff, "We're about to take off."

The boys played on the swings pretending to fly through space. Sally looked up at the sky and wondered how far it was to the Moon.

Just before four o'clock, Sally's mom called them in. It was almost time! Everyone gathered around the TV while Sally's dad adjusted the antenna to try to get a good picture.

The newscaster talked about the mission. Then, finally, they heard the astronauts and Mission Control in Houston, Texas. The newscaster said the astronauts' names were Neil Armstrong and Buzz Aldrin, who were aboard Apollo 11. On the screen was an image of the lunar module, the spacecraft the astronauts were traveling in on their way to the Moon. Fire shot out of the engines to make it move fast through space. Mrs. Grayson said the TV station had to recreate what was happening with models and animation.

"They can't have cameramen in space," she explained.

Sally couldn't understand a lot of what they were saying. The newscaster couldn't either. Mr. Grayson said it was a lot of technical information.

"Plus, the sound is coming from thousands of miles away, so it isn't as clear," he said.

"It's a really long long-distance phone call," Sally's mom said. "Imagine the cost of that one!"

Then, the TV station showed images of all the people watching TV at the airport, and even at Disneyland. Suddenly, they could see what was supposed to be the surface of the Moon. One of the newscasters said they were flying at the speed of 760 feet per second (or 231.65 meters per second).

"That's more than twice as long as a football field!" Sally said. And then the newscaster said it was slow for a space flight!

The next couple of minutes seemed to take forever. Finally, the astronaut announced, "The Eagle has landed." The module was on the surface of the Moon—about four and a half days after Apollo 11 took off!

Then, the man at Mission Control said, "You got a bunch of guys about to turn blue. We're breathing again. Thanks a lot."

Just then, Sally realized she had been holding her breath, too. Everyone clapped and laughed. Sally could even hear their neighbors clapping and shouting "Hooray!"

At dinner everyone talked about how amazing it was.

"When I was a little boy," Sally's dad said, "We could not have imagined such a thing!"

"The astronauts are heroes!" Jeff said.

"So are all the people at Mission Control," Sally said. "They kept the astronauts safe."

"And the entire world, millions of people, were watching together! Isn't that wonderful?" Mrs. Grayson said.

"I thought it was boring," Tommy said. "It was all beeps and numbers. We didn't even get to see the astronauts."

"That comes later when they do the moonwalk," Sally's dad said.

After dinner, the Graysons went home and Sally helped her mom clean up.

"Tommy and Jeff said I can't work at NASA because I'm a girl," Sally told her mom.

"Do you think that's true?" Sally's mom asked.

Sally shrugged her shoulders.

"I think Tommy and Jeff might not know as much as they think they do," her dad said.

Sally's parents said she and Tommy could stay up past their usual nine o'clock bedtime to watch the moonwalk, but by 9:30, Tommy said he was too tired and went to bed. Sally was so excited—she thought she might never sleep. Instead, she reread the day's newspaper stories about NASA while she waited for the next broadcast.

Finally, at 10:45, her dad turned on the TV again. Sally sat between her parents on the couch. Now, the TV was showing the astronauts, but it was actors recreating what was happening on the Moon. They were getting ready to step out of the lunar module. Sally moved to the floor to be closer to the TV. A piece of the fake lunar module unfolded from its side and then the image changed. The newscaster said the image was upside down. On the screen it said, "Live from the surface of the moon."

"Is that really them?" Sally asked, still staring at the TV screen.

"Yup," her mom said. "I can't believe it."

Sally couldn't believe it either. All the times she had looked up at the Moon, and now she was seeing its actual surface. They fixed the image so the picture was right-side up. She could see Neil Armstrong's feet coming down the steps. Sally asked her parents why it took so long for him to go down the steps.

"Gravity is different on the moon, and they have special, heavy suits. All that makes it hard for them to move," her dad said.

Finally, Mr. Armstrong stepped onto the surface of the Moon and said something. Although it was hard to hear at first, the newscaster made it clear for the audience. Neil Armstrong's first words on the Moon were "That's one small step for man, one giant leap for mankind." Sally could not stop staring at the TV.

The images on the screen were not clear. They looked more like shadows. But Sally was paying more attention to what Mr. Armstrong was saying. He described the surface of the Moon as powder and said his boots left prints in the layer of powder.

"Isn't this something?" the newscaster said. "They traveled 240,000 miles (about 386,243 kilometers) to get to the Moon. And we're seeing this!"

Sally ran to get her notebook. The Moon was 240,000 miles away, and she knew from watching the launch of the spacecraft that flew them to the Moon that it took them 76 hours to get there. With these numbers, she could figure out the average speed they traveled on the flight.

For the next two and a half hours, Sally and her parents watched as the astronauts collected rocks and did experiments on the Moon. They had their own camera with film to better document what they saw. They even talked to President Richard Nixon! It was midnight when it was done, and Sally was tired. But she knew her excitement would last.

The next morning, she was awake before her brother. Her dad was already in the kitchen. He was reading the newspaper and drinking coffee. On the front page of the newspaper in enormous letters it said, "MEN WALK ON THE MOON."

When her dad saw her, he said, "Here, Sally, look at this."

He opened the paper to a photo inside of all the people in Mission Control. He put the paper down on the table and pointed to one of the people.

"See there. That's a woman. Of course you can work at Mission Control. Just keep your grades up in math and science, and NASA will be lucky to have you! Don't let anyone tell you there's something you can't do because you are a girl."

"I already know the astronauts' average speed: 3,158 miles per hour (or 5,082 kilometers per hour) when they traveled to the moon," Sally said proudly. "Maybe one day I will help put the first man, or woman, on Mars!"

Key Words

1 **Use the Key Words to solve the riddles.**

a   I read the news on a TV show.
I tell you all that you need to know!

_____

c   I'm the machine that makes a car
go VROOOM! I can also send a
rocket to the Moon!

_____

b   I'm a scientific test that you can try.
Watch what happens and find
out why.

_____

d   This is what we do to send rockets into
the sky.
5, 4, 3, 2, 1 … look at them fly!

_____

Comprehension

2 **Read and circle _T_ (true), _F_ (false), or _DS_ (doesn't say).**

a President Kennedy kept his promise.	T	F	DS
b It was easy to understand what the astronauts were saying.	T	F	DS
c Neil Armstrong walked on the moon.	T	F	DS
d Women worked for NASA in the 1960s.	T	F	DS

3 **Match the numbers and dates with what they refer to.**

1   1969

2   240,000

3   3,158

a   average speed the spacecraft traveled in miles per hour

b   number of miles between the Earth and the moon

c   year of the first moon landing

4   **Match the causes with the effects.**

Cause ⟶ **Effect**

1   On July 20, 1969, the moon landing
was going to be on TV.

2   The sound of the astronauts' voices
came from thousands of miles away.

3   The astronaut announced, "The Eagle
has landed."

4   Gravity is different on the Moon.

a   They were difficult to understand.

b   Everybody clapped and cheered.

c   It was difficult for the astronauts
to move and walk down steps.

d   People took the day off work to
watch it.

Digging Deeper

5 🔊 **Read the causes and write the effects.**

a The surface of the Moon was like powder.

_____

_____

b The moon landing finished at midnight.

_____

_____

c Sally was very excited by the moon landing.

_____

_____

6 **Read the quotes from the story and write what they mean.**

a "The Eagle has landed."

_____

b "That's one small step for man, one giant leap for mankind."

_____

Personalization

7 **Write three events that a lot of people around the world watch on TV or on the Internet.**

_____

_____

_____

8 **Choose one event from Activity 7. Then, use adjectives from the box or use your own words to write a reason why you think so many people watch the event.**

amazing   scary   exciting   unbelievable
entertaining   interesting   important   funny

_____

_____

_____

5 What can history teach us?

Key Words

1 🎧 **Preview the Key Words.**
5.3

code (n)   replace   practical   talented

logical   influence (n)   original   calculator

2 **Match the definitions with the Key Words.**

1 to use something instead of something else   a logical

2 sensible or reasonable   b code

3 a machine or app used for adding, subtracting, etc. c replace

4 a set of letters, numbers, and symbols   d calculator

Pre-reading

3 **Look at the pictures on pages 71–73. Read the statements and mark (✔).**

Ada Lovelace ...	Yes, I agree.	No, I disagree.	I don't know.
a was born many years ago.			
b worked with scientists.			
c invented the laptop.			

4 🎧 **Listen and read.**
5.4

The First
Computer Programmer

By Kellie Dundon

Can you read the code?

Use the key to replace the symbols below with the correct word. Then, you can read the message!

KEY: % = just   **x** = code!   **>** = the   **@** = you   **$** = cracked

CODE: @ % $ > x

Ada Lovelace Shaped Your World

You might not have heard of her before, but Ada Lovelace shaped the world you live in. To understand how, let's look at what she and the world she lived in were like.

Ada Lovelace was a mathematician and writer. She lived from 1815 to 1852. There were no cars or ballpoint pens then! There were no airplanes, TVs, or movies. Kids didn't watch things or play games on their cell phones, tablets, or laptops. Why? Because none of these things had been invented!

Did you know?

Some of the latest inventions when Ada was born included gas lighting, photography, and steam engines. Imagine living in a world without computers, cars, airplanes, or electricity!

What invention would be hardest to live without?

Who Was Ada Lovelace?

Ada's mother wanted Ada to be practical. So Ada spent a lot more time than many other children studying math. Ada became *very* good at math. She was so talented that she worked with some of the most important scientists of the time. For example, she worked with Michael Faraday. His discoveries led to the electrical motor.

Ada became very practical and logical because of her mother's influence. But she was also creative like her father, Lord Byron. He was a famous poet. He wrote beautiful poetry using his imagination.

Ada believed it was important to use both her math skills and her creativity. That's how you can be original and invent new things!

The Father of Computers and the World's First Coder

Another important scientist Ada worked with was Charles Babbage. She met him in 1833. He told Ada about his idea to make a machine that could do math, like today's calculator apps. This is why he's often called the father of computers.

Ada was very excited. She understood how a machine could do math. She could also imagine how machines could do tasks that didn't use only numbers. She imagined that machines could work with other kinds of information, for example, letters or musical notes. And by doing that, she described what makes a computer a computer. It doesn't just do math. It saves, remembers, and follows steps.

The World's First Computer Coder

As Ada imagined, a computer could even write its own music!

Ada used her mathematical and her creative talents not only to describe how a computer could work. She also used those skills to invent the first series of steps a machine could read and respond to. These steps are very similar to the instructions or code that all computers use today. That's why some people call Ada the world's first computer coder!

Did you know?

All communication is code. Make up some sounds to replace words. Then, repeat them to the person next to you. Do they understand? For example, pretend that "Hum ho di dum" means "This is math class." Try it! Does your classmate understand what you mean? Probably not. Then, try saying "Math this is class" to your classmate. They probably still don't understand. That's because the words we use are a kind of code. Codes only work if we all know the same symbols. And we have to put the symbols in the right order. When we do that, we can communicate!

Thanks, Ada Lovelace!

Today, even small computers like cell phones, tablets, and laptops are everywhere. None of these could work without the kind of code Ada invented. So the next time you are playing your favorite computer game, remember it's possible thanks to the first computer coder, Ada Lovelace! And, the next time someone tells you that creative thinking is more important or that math is more important, you can tell them it's important to have both.

Ada wrote the first-ever computer code. Now people all over the world use computer code every day!

Key Words

1 Read the clues. Complete the crossword puzzle with the Key Words.

Down

1 the power to change or affect someone or something

Across

2 having a special ability to do something well

3 good at making decisions and sensible in daily life

4 not like others; new and different

Comprehension

2 Circle the correct options.

a Ada Lovelace was a mathematician and coder / artist and composer.

b Ada's father was Michael Faraday / Lord Byron.

c She believed it was important to combine math skills with poetry / creativity.

d She imagined how machines could work with only / more than numbers.

e The words we use are a kind of code / symbol.

f You can play computer games because of Ada Lovelace / your creative thinking.

3 Number the events in order.

a Ada spent more time than other children studying math.

b While she worked with Babbage, she created the first computer code.

c Now, cell phones, tablets, and laptops are everywhere.

d Ada was born in 1815.

e She started to work with a famous scientist named Charles Babbage.

f She died in 1852.

4 Mark (✔) the things that existed in Ada's lifetime.

ballpoint pens   photography   electricity   letters

steam engines   TVs   musical notes   phones

gas lighting   cars   candles   tablets

Digging Deeper

5 Complete the graphic organizer in your notebook.

Her father was the poet Lord Byron.

She described what makes a computer a computer.

Computer code is used in lots of devices.

She invented a series of steps a machine could read.

We can play video games.

She was born in 1815.

She was good at math.

She was practical and logical.

Skills and Abilities

Influence

Ada

Personal Details

Work

Personalization

6 Look at the code and solve the puzzle.

1 = A	2 = B	3 = C	4 = D	5 = E	6 = F	7 = G	8 = H	9 = I
10 = J	11 = K	12 = L	13 = M	14 = N	15 = O	16 = P	17 = Q	18 = R
19 = S	20 = T	21 = U	22 = V	23 = W	24 = X	25 = Y	26 = Z	

3	15	13	13	21	14	9	3	1	20	9	15	14

7 Write a sentence using the code in Activity 6 for a classmate to solve.

6 Where does food come from?

Key Words

1 🎧 **Preview the Key Words.**

6.1

savory   feast (n)   guru   crunchy

channel (n)   organic   traditional   hashtag

2 **Complete the sentences with the Key Words.**

a I like _____ snacks, like cheese and crackers.

b They are doing a folk dance wearing _____ clothes.

c She has a cooking TV show on _____ four. You can find her recipes online using this _____: #DianaCooks.

Pre-reading

3 **Look at the pictures on pages 77–81 and circle the correct options.**

a The story is about a boy / girl who learns how to cook / scuba dive.

b There are many types of food / animals in the story.

c The characters in the story are happy / sad.

4 🎧 **Listen and read.**

6.2

#AbuelaCooks

By Kellie Dundon • Illustrated by Daniela Martín del Campo

It was going to be the worst summer ever. Mom and Dad told me about a scuba diving vacation in Mexico, where Mom grew up. The problem was that *they* were the ones going scuba diving. I was going to stay with Abuela—that's Spanish for "Grandma"—in a small village in Mexico. The last time I was there, we didn't even have Internet access!

Don't misunderstand me—Abuela is amazing. She makes the most delicious Mexican food, and she gives the biggest hugs because she misses me most of the year. But my best friend Andy was going to spend the summer in Europe. And my friend Paula was going to New York! I was the only one who wasn't going to do anything interesting.

A week later, we had taken a plane, two buses, and a taxi to get to Abuela's house. The taxi shook as it drove over the cobblestone roads. Every house on the street was painted a different color. I ran up to Abuela's door to be the first one to get a hug.

"*Diego, mi amor!*" (Diego, my love!) she said and wrapped me in her arms. We all sat down to eat her delicious *tamales*. *Tamales* are dumplings made with corn flour. Abuela makes savory ones with meat and red sauce. And for dessert, she makes sweet *tamales* with lime and sugar.

Yesterday, Mom and Dad left. So now it's just Abuela and me. Well, Abuela, me, and lots of visitors. I think they just come over to the house to eat the feast she makes each day. Most of the time, I sit on the couch playing games. I check a video site for tips and Abuela looks over my shoulder.

"Is that your friend?"

"Who?"

"This one here, talking to you. Is that your friend?"

"No, Abuela. He's a YouTuber."

"What's a YouTuber?"

"YouTubers post videos on YouTube. They know about lots of different things, like video games, movies, art, makeup ... whatever. They're like gurus."

Abuela looks at the screen. "He is very young to be a guru. Come," she says, "put your YouGurus away and come to the market with me."

The local market isn't anything like where we buy groceries in San Diego. Abuela's market is outside. There are no shopping carts, barcodes, or cash registers—just colorful fresh produce, neatly piled in stands along the street. We pass someone selling little bags of reddish-brown snacks. "Try one!" Abuela says. I pick one up and pop it in my mouth. It's crunchy and salty.

"Yum! What is it?"

"Fried crickets," she says with a big smile.

"Insects?!"

She buys a small bag of them from the lady and gives it to me. Maybe I'll try just one more.

At the market, they call Abuela *Doña Elsa*—that means Lady Elsa. It sounds so formal and polite. She points to all the things she wants, with both hands, like she's conducting an orchestra. The market vendors weigh the food. When they tell her it costs 20 pesos, she says it should be ten, so they sell it to her for 15 pesos. They both smile, like it's a game. I've never seen *that* happen at the supermarket at home.

Later on, at her house, I'm playing the best round of Jungle Slayer in my life when I hear a cry. I drop my tablet and run to see what has happened. Abuela is holding her hand under running cold water. She says the neighbor's cat bit her, but not too hard. I remembered a first-aid channel I'd seen on YouTube a while ago. I run to get the first-aid kit. Abuela watches me in surprise.

"You say you learned to do this a year ago? And you still remember?"

"Sure, I guess so."

After I clean and cover the wound, Abuela says, "Come to the kitchen. We have lots of cooking to do."

"I don't know how to cook! I'm ten!"

"Well, I can't cook with my sore hand. You're ten, but I'm 60. With my head and your body, we can cook!"

In the kitchen, there are chopped organic tomatoes, corn kernels, avocados, and freshly cut bright green limes. I can see tortillas in three different colors!

Now, this is where it gets a bit crazy. Abuela starts pointing to things and telling me long sentences about what to do … in Spanish! And, oh boy, she is bossy in the kitchen! It's a lot of work, but it's also a lot of fun. Abuela watches me and says, "If only your mother could cook our country's food like this!"

The next day, I have an idea. "Abuela, wait here!" I run to get my tablet. When she sees it, she shakes her finger in the air. "No GameGuru now! We are cooking!"

"No, Abuela, you don't understand. I'm going to make you a YouTuber!"

She's too distracted tasting our red rice to listen. So I set up the tablet so we're both visible on the screen and hit the record button. "Today, we're making *mole*," she says.

"What's that?"

"*Mole* is a traditional Mexican sauce with a lot, and I mean A LOT, of ingredients. Our recipe uses chocolate, chili, tomatoes, dried fruits, spices, and nuts. Every family has secret ingredients. We crush all the ingredients together until we have a powder, or a paste. That's *mole*. Then, we can cook meat in it."

Abuela claps her hands. "Let's cook!"

For the next hour, she shouts orders at me in Spanish, waving her arms. We make the best *mole* sauce. And I record the funniest *mole* cooking lesson ever. I upload it to YouTube and send the link to Mom and some of my friends. The next day, I record Abuela's *tamales*-making lesson. The day after, I record her making peppers stuffed with meat and nuts, and a cream sauce on top.

It's almost the end of my vacation in Mexico. I check my tablet to see if Mom has watched the cooking lessons. I nearly drop the tablet when I see the screen! There are more than 3,000 likes! I guess people think Abuela is as much fun as I do! A lot of people are trying her recipes and posting the photos. Someone has even given her a hashtag: #AbuelaCooks.

The next time we go to the market, some tourists see us, and one yells out, "Look, it's AbuelaCooks!" A week after that, Abuela and I are interviewed on a morning TV show. And now that I'm back at school, everyone keeps asking about my famous Abuela!

So I guess my summer wasn't so bad after all. Abuela tells me it wasn't becoming a "YouGuru" that makes her so proud. She's proud because her grandson showed the whole world how to cook the food of our ancestors.

Key Words

1 Read the definitions and write the Key Words.

a *adjective* hard and making a loud noise when eaten ___ ___ ___ ___ ___ ___ ___

b *adjective* grown without artificial chemicals ___ ___ ___ ___ ___ ___ ___

c *noun* a person who knows a lot about a particular subject ___ ___ ___ ___

d *noun* a special meal with large amounts of food and drinks ___ ___ ___ ___ ___

Comprehension

2 Circle the correct option to complete the questions. Then, write the answers.

a **Where** / **Who** is going to New York for the summer?

_____

b **Who** / **What** are *tamales*?

_____

c **Where** / **What** do Abuela and Diego buy groceries?

_____

d **How** / **Why** old are Diego and Abuela?

_____

e **What** / **When** does Diego check his tablet to see if Mom watched the video?

_____

f **Why** / **Who** are Abuela and Diego interviewed on TV?

_____

3 List the ingredients for each of the following dishes in the story.

a Savory *tamales* _____

b *Mole* _____

4 Read and write *D* (Diego) or *A* (Abuela).

a gives great hugs ☐   d plays a computer game ☐

b eats something for the first time ☐   e knows first aid ☐

c gets bitten by a cat ☐   f knows people at the market ☐

Digging Deeper

5 📖 Write questions about something in the story you want to know more about. Then, research the information and write the answers.

| Why … ? | How … ? | Who … ? | What … ? |

What other traditional foods are from Mexico? _____

_____

_____

_____

6 Read the section of the story on pages 80–81 again. Then, complete the graphic organizer.

#AbuelaCooks Chain of Events

This happened …

> A cat bites Abuela's hand.

Causing this to happen …

Finally, this happened …

Personalization

7 Describe a YouTuber you watch or want to watch.

a What's the name of the YouTuber or program? _____

b What is it about? _____

c Why do you like it? _____

8 Imagine you are a YouTuber. Give yourself a hashtag name. Be inventive!

_____

6 Where does food come from?

Key Words

1 🎧 6.3 **Preview the Key Words.**

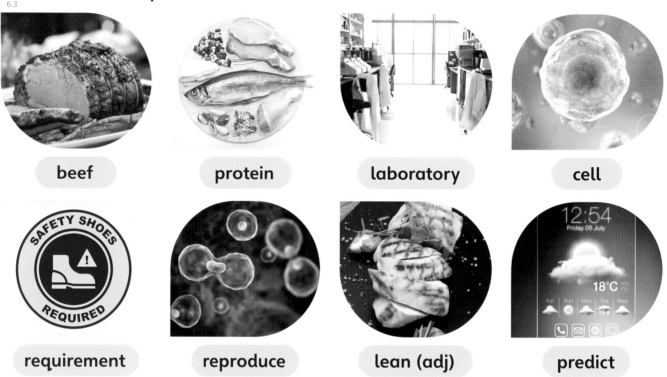

| beef | protein | laboratory | cell |

| requirement | reproduce | lean (adj) | predict |

2 **Read the glossary entries and write the Key Words.**

a _____ *noun* something that is needed

b _____ *noun* a place where science experiments are done

c _____ *noun* a very small part that forms all living things

d _____ *verb* to make a copy of something; to make a baby

Pre-reading

3 📖 **Look at the pictures and read the captions on pages 85–87. Then, mark (✔) the themes of the article.**

a The effects on the environment caused by eating meat ☐

b Burgers made from vegetables ☐

c Buying a new kind of meat ☐

d Making meat in a laboratory ☐

4 🎧 6.4 **Listen and read.**

Are You Ready to Try ... Meat Made in a Laboratory?

By Susana Ramírez Félix

Do you love a juicy hamburger? Have you ever considered not eating meat? Would it be easy or difficult for you to stop eating it?

Some people worry about the negative effects that raising animals for meat has on our planet. Others worry that animals suffer. And some say there will not be enough food to feed everyone. All these things have inspired people to look for new ways to produce meat.

Environmental destruction caused by meat production

Did you know?

An estimated 15,944 liters of water are needed to produce just one kilogram of beef. This is what is called the water footprint of beef production.

Raising animals for meat pollutes the environment and uses up valuable resources. It causes a huge amount of greenhouse gas emissions. Approximately a quarter of the world's land is used to produce food for the livestock that gives us meat. That means we cut down forests and there are fewer trees to make oxygen.

In addition, researchers say that we eat four times more food than we did 50 years ago. In 2018, people around the world ate about 59 billion kilograms of beef. By 2050, specialists say we will need around 455 billion kilograms per year to feed everyone! Can you imagine all the land and water we will need to produce that much meat? Think of all the damage this does to the environment!

If we continue eating as much meat as we are eating now, there soon will not be enough land or water to feed the animals. By 2050, there will be enough food to feed only half of the world's population!

Instead, the land and water that is being used to raise animals could be used to grow plants. That way we would have enough plant-based food, like fruits and vegetables, and do much less damage to the planet. Easy, right?

Well, no. Many people around the world like meat and want to keep eating it. They say it tastes delicious, and they like it better than fruits and vegetables. Or at least they don't want to *only* eat plants. Meat also has a lot of nutrients, like proteins, fat, and minerals. It can be hard to get enough of those nutrients in plant-based foods. That is especially the case with iron, which we need for our blood. Meat has iron, but not a lot of plants do.

If we can't or don't want to give up meat, what can we do?

The answer might be to make meat in a laboratory! Around a decade ago, scientists started to think about how to produce real meat that uses fewer resources and without harming the environment so much. They came up with the idea of cell-based meat.

Making meat in a lab

What is cell-based meat? Well, it's exactly what it sounds like—meat that grows from meat cells like any other meat. But, instead of growing in an animal on a farm, it grows in a laboratory. Imagine eating a hamburger, and, while you are eating it, the cow the meat comes from could still be alive, looking at you! Although it might sound a little bit weird, it's not science fiction. In 2013, scientists produced the first burger made from cell-based meat.

How is cell-based meat produced?

There are four basic requirements to grow cell-based meat:

1 A sample of cells from an animal—this sample only has to be the size of a sesame seed, but it contains millions of cells that can reproduce many times.
2 Something the cells can stick to.
3 Some food for the cells to "eat" so they grow and reproduce themselves.
4 Something for the meat to grow in.

Looks like meat, tastes like meat!

Specialists say that this cell-based meat tastes the same as lean meat we get from traditional sources because it is, well, meat. The only difference is that it does not grow like a muscle of an animal, it grows in a lab. We'd no longer need to hurt an animal to eat its meat. We just have to borrow some of its cells. We'd no longer need to use up so much land for farm animals. We wouldn't use thousands of liters of water. And we wouldn't generate so much pollution. That's why cell-based meat is also called clean meat.

It sounds pretty good, right? So, what are we waiting for? Some companies say they are ready to sell cell-based meat in markets around the world. They are just waiting for the governments to approve it. Scientists predict that cell-based meat will be found in stores by 2022. Are you ready to try it?

Coming to a store near you!

Key Words

1 Find the Key Words. Then, complete the sentences.

P	T	Z	B	D	I	P
R	R	X	M	V	R	R
E	D	C	L	R	Q	O
D	F	B	E	E	F	T
I	C	B	A	R	M	E
C	W	D	N	H	Q	I
T	V	W	T	A	F	N

a _____ is the meat from a cow.

b The doctor told me I can eat _____ meat—meat without fat.

c There is a lot of _____ in meat, milk, eggs, and beans.

d The weather forecasters can _____ the temperature.

Comprehension

2 Match the sentence halves.

1 One quarter of the world's land ...

2 We eat four times more food ...

3 It is difficult to get enough nutrients ...

4 To grow cell-based meat, ...

a than we did 50 years ago.

b is used to raise livestock.

c from plant-based foods.

d you need cells from an animal.

3 Circle the correct option to answer the questions.

1 What is the name for the amount of water we use to produce beef?

  a water production   b water footprint   c water emissions

2 By 2050, how many people in the world will not have enough food?

  a 50 percent   b all of them   c those who don't eat meat

3 What do we need to grow cell-based meat?

  a sesame seeds   b iron   c a container

4 Read the article on pages 85–87 again. Circle the author's purpose.

a The author wants to give you facts about how much meat we need to eat.

b The author wants to make you think about the advantages of cell-based meat.

c The author wants to encourage you to stop eating all types of meat.

d The author wants to show you how to buy cell-based meat.

Digging Deeper

5 Complete the Venn diagram.

| tastes like meat | uses a lot of water | grows in a lab |
| grows on an animal | doesn't use land | contains animal cells |

Cell-Based Meat   Both   Meat

6 🔖 Circle the correct option to complete each sentence.

I   The author of the article says that regular meat is …

    a   delicious.   b   bad for the environment.   c   expensive.

2   The author of the article says that cell-based meat is …

    a   not tasty.   b   good for the environment.   c   in stores now.

7 Write three advantages of cell-based meat.

a   _____

b   _____

c   _____

Personalization

8 Do you think cell-based meat is a good idea? Why or why not?

_____

_____

9 Do you want to try cell-based meat? Why or why not?

_____

_____

7 Why is water important?

Key Words

1 **Preview the Key Words.**
7.1

in trouble

ashamed

horrified

maze

beneath

sink (v)

fishermen

monument

2 Read the definitions and mark (✔) the correct Key Word.

a showing or feeling great shock   ☐ ashamed   ☐ horrified

b a place that has many confusing paths   ☐ maze   ☐ beneath

c to go below the surface of the water   ☐ monument   ☐ sink

d having a serious problem   ☐ in trouble   ☐ ashamed

Pre-reading

3 Look at the pictures on pages 91–95 and circle the correct options.

What type of text is it?	Where does it happen?	When does it take place?
science fiction	on another planet	in the past
a myth	in a king or queen's palace	in the present
a fable with animals	at sea	in the future

4   **Listen and read.**
7.2

The Nereids

A Greek myth adapted by Jeremy Edgar • Illustrated by Yaritza Andrade

At the bottom of the ocean, in a golden palace, lived an ancient god. Older than even Poseidon, Nereus was called the Old Man of the Sea. He took care of all the waters on Earth, as well as all the creatures who lived in the waters. Nereus married Doris, a kind and gentle sea nymph. Nereus and Doris had 50 daughters who were called the Nereids. The Nereids were beautiful and kind like their mother, and each one had a special duty. Kymo created waves and Neso was in charge of the islands. Their leader was called Thetis. Thetis took care of all the fish.

When Poseidon became the god of the sea, he fell in love with Amphitrite, the Nereid who calms storms. She married Poseidon and became the queen of the sea.

The Nereids were always friendly and helpful. If a ship was in trouble because of a storm, Kymo would calm the waves. If fishermen hadn't caught any fish and their families were hungry, Leagore took them to the fish so that they could catch them.

There are many stories about the Nereids helping Greek heroes. One of the most famous is the time they helped Theseus save the children from the Minotaur.

Theseus was the son of King Aegeus of Athens. Every year, the king sent seven girls and seven boys to King Minos of Crete. One year, when Theseus was still young, he asked his father, "Why do we send these children to Crete?"

"Because King Minos is very powerful," his father answered. "If we don't send them, he will attack Athens and destroy us."

"And why don't we ever see these children again?" Theseus asked.

The king looked ashamed. "Well, son," he said, "King Minos has a pet monster. It is called the Minotaur. It is half man and half bull, and it scares the children and puts them in prison."

Theseus was horrified. He thought for a minute and then said, "I want you to send me with the children, and I will kill this monster."

So, that year, Theseus went with the other children to Crete. The Minotaur lived in the middle of an underground maze. It was King Minos's habit to send the children into the maze one at a time. When the children arrived in Crete, the King selected a girl to go into the maze first.

"No!" Theseus shouted. "I will go into the maze first!"

King Minos was surprised. "Who are you to tell a king what to do?" he asked the young hero.

So Theseus decided to fool King Minos and replied, "My name is Theseus and I am the son of Poseidon."

King Minos laughed. He didn't believe Theseus. Then, he thought of an impossible test for the young prince. He removed a gold ring from his finger and threw it into the ocean.

"If you are really the son of Poseidon, go to the bottom of the ocean and bring me my ring." Then, the wicked king pushed Theseus into the ocean.

The Nereids had been watching all of this from the ocean and knew what was happening. As soon as Theseus was beneath the waves, he was surrounded by Nereids who were riding on dolphins.

"Come with us," they told Theseus.

Theseus climbed on a dolphin and followed the Nereids to their spectacular palace at the bottom of the ocean. The Nereids explained everything to their father. When Nereus heard the story, he welcomed Theseus into his palace. The Nereids gave Theseus the ring, and Nereus gave him a golden crown to show King Minos. Theseus then went back to King Minos. When the king saw the ring and the crown, he was afraid of Theseus.

"OK," he told Theseus. "You can go into the maze first and meet the Minotaur!"

And that is how, thanks to the Nereids, Theseus killed the Minotaur and saved the children of Athens.

The Nereids are also famous for helping other heroes. Jason and the Argonauts had many adventures, but the most dangerous of these was to sail between the Moving Rocks. Whenever a ship tried to sail between these rocks, the rocks came together and crushed it. Hera, the wife of Zeus, liked Jason. She knew that the Argonauts could not survive the Moving Rocks without help. So she asked the Nereids to help.

When the Nereids found the Argonauts, they were resting on a beach. They were afraid to sail through the Moving Rocks. However, Thetis convinced Jason to try. And when their ship got near the rocks, the waves got higher and higher—soon the Argonauts were sailing though a violent storm. The waves threw the ship high into the air like a toy. Then, just when the Argonauts thought that their ship would sink, the Nereids appeared. They swam around the ship, laughing and jumping out of the water like dolphins playing. The storm raged, but the waters around the ship stayed calm thanks to the Nereids. At that point, the rocks began to move. Closer and closer they came. When they were about to crush the ship, the Nereids lifted the boat out of the water and carried it through the deadly passage. The ship and the Argonauts were safe!

The Nereids didn't only help heroes. These water nymphs were always watching from the oceans and the rivers, and were ready to help when needed.

One time, there was an island that was in trouble. The weather there was stormy. The fishermen couldn't go out in their boats, and the people were hungry. Neso called her sisters, and they swam out to help.

Leagore brought a large school of fish with her. With the help of Maira, she took the fish up a river so the people could fish in safety. However, a small girl tried to catch one of the fish and fell into the river. Maira immediately swam to the girl. She caught the child and gently handed her to her grateful mother. Melite then calmed the seas around the island so that the fishermen could sail out safely.

The people of the island never forgot about the Nereids. They built a monument in their honor. Visitors to the island saw the monument and heard the story of how the Nereids had helped the people of the island. Then, when the visitors returned to their own island, they also built monuments so that the Nereids would help them whenever they had a problem with the rivers or ocean.

Key Words

1 **Read the clues. Complete the crossword puzzle with the Key Words.**

Across

1 The ___ went out to sea in their boats.

3 The king feels embarrassed and ___ about the children he sends to Minos.

4 The ship sank ___ the waves.

Down

2 The islanders built a ___ for the Nereids.

Comprehension

2 **Read and circle *T* (true) or *F* (false).**

a The Nereids kept fishermen safe and helped them find food.   T   F

b King Aegeus sent 14 children to Crete to kill the Minotaur.   T   F

c King Minos decided to test the Nereids.   T   F

d Zeus helped Jason and the Argonauts survive the Moving Rocks.   T   F

e The Nereids stopped Jason's ship from sinking.   T   F

f The Greek gods built monuments to honor the Nereids.   T   F

3 **Use the names of the characters from the story to solve the riddles.**

a We can swim like dolphins in stormy water or calm. Fast beneath the waves, we protect you from harm.

b You should be afraid of me, for I'm an evil king. I'll send you to the Minotaur or make you find my ring.

c I'm a famous adventurer, and the Nereids saved my life. I passed by the Moving Rocks, thanks to Zeus's wife!

Digging Deeper

4 Complete the graphic organizer.

	Theseus and the Minotaur	Jason and the Moving Rocks
a **Problem**		
b **How the Nereids helped**		
c **Result**		

5 📖 Read and circle the sequence words and time expressions. Then, number the events in order.

a Then, a girl fell in the river, and Maira went to get her. ☐

b When Neso heard this, she called her sisters to help. ☐

c Finally, Melite calmed the seas so the fishermen could catch fish safely. ☐

d One day, there was a storm on an island. ☐

e First, Leagore and Maira took a school of fish up the river. ☐

f After she rescued her, Maira handed the child to her mother. ☐

g As a result, the fishermen couldn't go out on their boats and the people got hungry. ☐

Personalization

6 Imagine you have special powers to help people. What three things can you do?

a _____

b _____

c _____

7 Why is water important?

Key Words

1 🎧 **Preview the Key Words.**
7.3

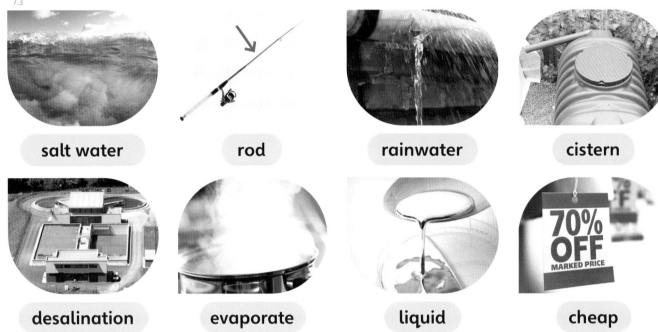

salt water   rod   rainwater   cistern

desalination   evaporate   liquid   cheap

2 **Read and write the Key Words.**

a A fishing _____ is a stick used to catch fish.

b Water can _____, or turn to vapor, at room temperature.

c A _____ is a container used to save water. It is like a big tank.

d It's good to collect _____ and use it to water the plants.

Pre-reading

3 **Look at the pictures on pages 99–101. Use your background knowledge to circle the correct answers.**

a Water covers 70% / 97% of the Earth's surface.

b We can only drink salt water / fresh water.

c People have collected rainwater for hundreds / thousands of years.

d A drought is when it doesn't rain / rains for a long time.

e There won't be any / will be more water problems in the world very soon.

4 🎧 **Listen and read.**
7.4

Running Dry

By Robert Gareth Vaughan

Your body depends on it. Plants and animals do, too. The clothes you wear, the food you eat, and the cell phone you use are all made with it. What is this magical, valuable ingredient? Water, of course! But will this essential element to all life on Earth run out?

The simple answer is "no." Scientists believe that the water on Earth is over four billion years old. (That's about the same age as the Sun!) And it will probably be around for the rest of Earth's life. But this is salt water. And we can't drink salt water because it contains salt, which makes us sick.

Water covers nearly 70% of the Earth's surface, and about 97% of all the water on Earth is in the ocean.

Amazing Water Fact

All the water on Earth came from comets and asteroids!

Fresh water is the water we can drink. It only makes up 2.5% of the water on Earth, and most of it isn't available because it's trapped in glaciers. This is the kind of water that may run out. But why? Well, there are a lot of reasons. Three of the main ones are the increasing population, climate change, and agriculture. The problem is a very serious one. But don't worry! Scientists are now looking for ways to produce fresh water.

Amazing Water Fact

Some of the water that you drink is the same water that dinosaurs once drank.

Did you know?

People in the 16th century used to look for water with sticks. And some people still do! This is called "divining." The stick—or "divining rod"—looks like the letter Y. The person searching for water holds it in both hands and walks on land where they think there is water. If the rod moves, there could be water there. Nobody knows if this really works. But there are other more efficient ways of finding fresh water. Let's look at some of them.

One of the oldest (and cheapest) ways to have fresh water is to collect rainwater. People have done this for centuries. There is evidence that people made rainwater collection systems in 2000 BCE in India and China! In Istanbul, Turkey, a large cistern was built under the city in the 6th century. Hundreds of years later, many cities are copying Turkey. In Melbourne, Australia, there is a container that can hold about four million liters of rainwater!

It's easy to collect rainwater! Connect a water pipe to your roof and put a container below.

The Basilica Cistern in Istanbul, which no longer contains water, is a popular tourist attraction. This is one of hundreds of cisterns underneath the city.

Amazing Water Fact

It takes 140 liters of water to grow, process, and transport the coffee beans for a single cup of coffee.

We can also turn the water we *can't* drink into water we *can* drink. This is called desalination. That means taking the salt out of salt water to make fresh water. This happens naturally when water in the ocean evaporates. But we can make it happen, too, in huge factories. This is an excellent solution because there is so much water in the oceans that it will never run out. But there are disadvantages to desalination. The buildings and machines are very expensive. Poorer countries don't have enough money to build them.

The process also uses a lot of energy. And some of this energy may come from fossil fuels, which create pollution. The waste from desalination contains a lot of salt and chemicals. And this often goes back into the ocean and damages marine plants and animals.

A drought is when it doesn't rain for a very, very long time. Droughts are becoming more common all over the world. But what if we could make our own rain? Sounds like something from a sci-fi movie, right? Believe it or not, we already can! This is called cloud seeding, and governments have done it for years.

What does cloud seeding involve? Water in clouds needs salt or dust so it can change from a gas into a liquid and fall as rain. But there isn't much salt and dust in the atmosphere. So, airplanes drop chemicals similar to salt and dust onto clouds to make it rain.

Amazing Water Fact

China used cloud seeding to keep rain away from the 2008 Beijing Olympics opening ceremony. How? They made it rain in other areas while the ceremony was taking place!

Cloud seeding helps areas where there are droughts. It also makes it easier to grow crops. But there are disadvantages. The chemicals can harm the environment. It's also not certain that cloud seeding really works. It's mostly used on clouds that are already going to produce rain anyway, and it may also change the weather in areas close by. And, like desalination, it isn't cheap.

Fresh water is critical for a healthy life, and these are just some of the solutions that could provide the fresh water we need. But will they solve the problem? At the present rate we are using water, the answer, unfortunately, is no—and the situation could get worse. According to the World Wildlife Fund, very soon, two thirds of the world's population might not have enough water. It's important to start using our water more efficiently and effectively to prevent our sources of fresh water from running dry.

Key Words

1 **Unscramble the Key Words and complete the sentences.**

| w-t-r-e-a a-l-t-s   n-i-i-n-a-o-t-l-a-s-e-d   q-i-d-u-i-l   a-p-e-h-c |

a   The _____ process is when we take the salt out of water from the ocean.

b   Cloud seeding helps change gas into _____.

c   The machines for desalinating water aren't _____. In fact, they are very expensive!

d   Nearly 97% of the water on Earth is in the ocean. It is _____.

2 **Answer the questions.**

a   **Where** does Earth's water come from?

_____

b   **Why** did people use divining rods?

_____

c   **How** much water does the cistern in Melbourne hold?

_____

d   **What** does cloud seeding do?

_____

e   **What** do cloud seeding and desalination have in common?

_____

3 **Complete the summary of the article.**

| making   drink   worse   collecting   solutions   salt water |

Most of the Earth's water is salt water that we cannot **(1)** _____.

We need fresh water to survive. We can have more fresh water water by

(2) _____ it in cisterns, making it from **(3)** _____

through desalination, or **(4)** _____ rain by cloud seeding.

However, our water problems are likely to get **(5)** _____.

We need to find practical **(6)** _____.

Digging Deeper

4 🗣 **Find and underline evidence in the article on pages 99–101 that supports the following points. Then, write the evidence in the graphic organizer.**

Point	Evidence
a Fresh water is likely to run out.	Example: _____ _____ _____
b People have collected rainwater for centuries.	Example: _____ _____ _____
c Governments already practice cloud seeding.	Example: _____ _____ _____

5 **Complete the graphic organizer.**

Technique	Advantages	Disadvantages
a Desalination		
b Cloud Seeding		

Personalization

6 **Read the final sentence from the article and list three ways you can use water more efficiently.**

"It's important to start using our water more efficiently and effectively to prevent our sources of fresh water from running dry."

a _____

b _____

c _____

8 How do numbers shape our lives?

Key Words

1 🎧 **Preview the Key Words.**
8.1

fraction   bother (v)   slice (n)   stuck

hold on   height   bend over   calculate

2 Complete the sentences with the Key Words.

a The boy is _____ in the tree. How can we help him? He can't _____ much longer.

b What is your _____? I'm 140 centimeters tall.

c You can use a cake to learn about _____. For example, if you cut it in two, one _____ is half of the cake.

Pre-reading

3 Look at the pictures on pages 105–III and circle the correct options.

a The story is about a boy / girl who is good at sports / math.

b The story begins at school / in a park.

c The characters in the story are all children / children and adults.

4 🎧 **Listen and read.**
8.2

Meghan's Math Saves the Day!

By Kim Milne • Illustrated by Javier Montiel

It was a typical day in Meghan's 4th grade math class ...

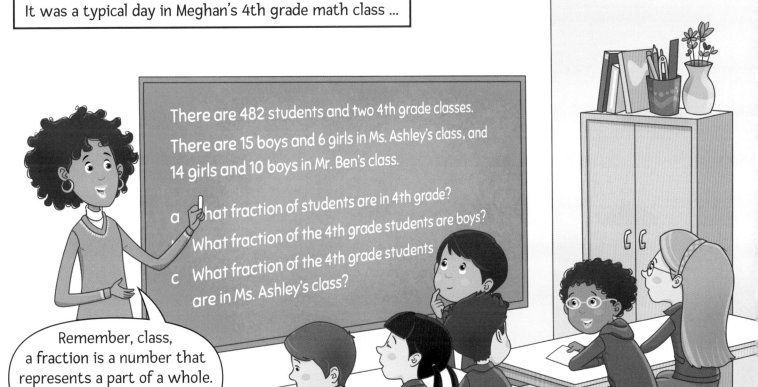

There are 482 students and two 4th grade classes.
There are 15 boys and 6 girls in Ms. Ashley's class, and 14 girls and 10 boys in Mr. Ben's class.

a What fraction of students are in 4th grade?

b What fraction of the 4th grade students are boys?

c What fraction of the 4th grade students are in Ms. Ashley's class?

Remember, class, a fraction is a number that represents a part of a whole. Now, who can solve the problems first?

When will I ever use this stuff?

Good job, Meghan!

a. 45/482

b. 5/9

c. 7/15

After school, Meghan and Tyrone ride home through the park.

Look at the spirals in this pine cone! They go around in a circle. And they spread out, like fireworks.

Awesome!

And, if you count the spirals, they follow the Fibonacci Sequence. You know ... 0, 1, 1, 2, 3, 5, 8, 13, 21, 34 ...

Look at this buttercup flower! The number of leaves and petals is a Fibonacci number. It has 5 petals!

And this corn marigold has 13 petals!

Wow! I thought that math happened only in the classroom.

Just then, the twins Bruce and Brandon ride by.

Are you counting daisies Meghan? Ha-ha!

Don't pay any attention to them, Meghan.

Key Words

1 Find the Key Words. Then, complete the definitions.

S	A	Z	F	D	I	F	G	T	V	Q
H	R	O	R	S	L	I	C	E	P	S
E	D	C	A	L	C	U	L	A	T	E
I	F	B	C	N	L	J	E	T	Z	R
G	N	V	T	N	T	O	R	A	R	P
H	A	B	I	R	D	E	T	L	B	Z
T	V	B	O	T	H	E	R	N	Q	V
T	I	P	N	O	V	I	D	E	T	L
R	Q	S	T	U	C	K	B	R	A	Z

a   a number that represents a part of a whole _____

b   a piece that is cut from a pie or cake _____

c   to discover an amount or number using math _____

d   to annoy or worry

_____

e   a measurement of how tall something is _____

f   not able to move _____

Comprehension

2 Mark (✔) the ways Meghan uses math in the story.

a   to study flowers ☐

b   to solve a math problem in class ☐

c   to calculate the cost of a pizza ☐

d   to help do her friend's homework ☐

e   to calculate the height of a tree ☐

f   to help place the ladder for Brandon correctly ☐

g   to add up how many cakes the school cafeteria needs each week ☐

h   to get a ball from a tree ☐

3 Answer the questions.

a   What does Meghan use to calculate the cost of a slice of pizza? _____

b   Who is one of Meghan's heroes? _____

c   How much does a pizza cost if you buy five separate slices? _____

d   How many petals does a corn marigold have? _____

e   Who gets stuck in a tree? _____

f   What shape does Meghan use to calculate the height of the tree? _____

Digging Deeper

4 **Reread the pages below and circle the best page summary.**

1 Page 108

    a Meghan shows Tyrone a pine cone and flowers, and Tyrone becomes interested in nature.

    b Meghan shows Tyrone a pine cone and flowers, and Tyrone becomes more interested in math.

2 Page 110

    a Meghan uses what she knows about ladders to calculate the height of the tree.

    b Meghan calculates the height of the tree by using Pythagoras' theorem.

5 **Read the story on pages 105–111 again. Then, complete the graphic organizer.**

Settings	Characters

Beginning	Middle	End

Personalization

6 **How do you use math each day? Match the activity with its math application.**

1 waking up	a measuring ingredients
2 shopping	b setting the alarm clock for a specific time
3 cooking and/or eating	c trying on clothes in a store by size

7 **Write three more daily activities and how you apply math to each.**

a _____

b _____

c _____

8 **How do numbers shape our lives?**

Key Words

1 🎧 Preview the Key Words.
8.3

length   weight   measurement   pace (n)

metric system   equal to   scale   equator

2 Read the glossary entries and write the Key Words.

scale   length   weight   pace

a _____ *noun* the distance from one end of something to the other

b _____ *noun* how heavy something is

c _____ *noun* a single step or the length of a step

d _____ *noun* a device for weighing people or things

Pre-reading

3 What do you know about the metric system? Complete the graphic organizer.

What I Know	What I Want to Know
_____	_____
_____	_____
_____	_____

4 🎧 Listen and read.
8.4

Measures, Measures Everywhere!

By Keila Ochoa

This is Lucas. He works at the market selling fruit and vegetables. Lucas measures his daily routine in terms of **length** or distance, **weight**, and time.

How Do We Measure Length or Distance?

In the past, the Egyptians used fingers and arms to measure objects. They used the length of a person's arm, from the elbow to the tip of the middle finger. They called this a cubit.

Amazing History!

The Great Pyramid of Giza in Egypt is 400 cubits per side and 280 cubits high. But whose arm was used to determine the **measurement**? The King of Ancient Egypt's arm, of course!

Greeks and Romans measured things using the foot. Roman armies walked very far, so a Roman mile was 1,000 paces. A pace is a single step taken when walking or running. The problem was that every person's foot is a different size and the length of every person's pace varies. That made this system of measurement hard to use!

In Ancient China, body parts were also used to measure length. Around 220 BCE, Emperor Qin Shi Huang decided to standardize measurement—that means that there was one measuring system for everyone. He used a decimal system, so each unit was ten times bigger than the one before. The concept was similar to the metric system today.

Around 1100 in England, King Henry I defined the length from his nose to his thumb as a measuring unit. He called it a yard. A yard is equal to three feet. This system is called the imperial system. The imperial system is still used in countries such as the United States, Myanmar, and Liberia.

Today, most countries use the metric system. The metric system we use today was developed in France in the 1790s. The measurements in the metric system are based on the natural world, such as the size of the Earth. The metric system uses a decimal system based on multiples of ten. That makes it very easy to use!

Lucas lives in Brazil, where they use the metric system. His home is 11 kilometers from the market where he works. How far is your home from school?

How Do We Measure Weight?

A very long time ago, Lucas might have weighed a tomato in one hand and an apple in the other hand to estimate which was heavier.

Today Lucas uses a scientific instrument to weigh the fruit and vegetables that he sells. Do you know what that is? The **scale**!

Ancient civilizations also used scales to weigh things. They used different weights on scales. First, they used grains. They put grains on one side of the scale and the object they wanted to weigh on the other side. Later, they used stones!

In the United States, you can buy a pound of tomatoes. In the rest of the world, people use the metric system, or kilograms, to weigh things.

Lucas weighs some mangoes using kilograms. A kilogram is equal to the weight of one liter of water. Do you know how many kilograms you weigh?

How Do We Measure Time?

We use calendars to keep track of time. Calendars help us organize and plan our lives. Modern calendars measure a solar year—that's the time it takes for the Earth to make a complete circuit around the Sun.

Measuring Time: The Calendar

In the Roman Empire, Julius Caesar determined the number of days in a year to be 365 and a quarter. In 1582, Pope Gregory corrected this calendar. He added a leap year to make it work. Every four years is a leap year. That means there is one extra day at the end of February.

Amazing History!
The calendar we use has a 27-second error every year! Did you know that the calendar used by Mayans in Mexico has only a 13-second error?

Lucas sells tomatoes in late summer. In Brazil, summer is from December through March. That is because Brazil is south of the **equator**. In your country, when is summer?

Measuring Time: Clock, Sundial, and Hourglass

We use clocks to measure days, or the time it takes the Earth to make a complete turn on its own axis. All countries in the world measure time in the same way.

a sundial

Older civilizations used a number system based on 12 and 60, not 10. For that reason, Egyptians divided the day into 24 parts. These were hours. The Babylonians then divided one hour into 60 minutes, and a minute into 60 seconds.

But what instruments were used to measure time before the invention of mechanical clocks? People used to use sundials. The sun's shadow moves around a dial divided by hours. But this didn't work very well on cloudy days! In the Middle Ages, they used the hourglass.

an hourglass

It's 5 p.m. Lucas is now ready to drive 11 kilometers to his home. It will take him 15 minutes to get there. He sold 56 kilograms of fruits and vegetables, and worked for about 32,400 seconds! What a day!

Key Words

1 **Use the Key Words to solve the riddles.**

a It's easy to calculate with me because you use multiples of ten, for example: 1,000 meters = 1 kilometer. Easy, right?

_____

c Length in meters or paces, weight in kilograms and pounds, and time in minutes and seconds. You use me every day.

_____

b I divide Earth into two equal parts: the Northern Hemisphere and the Southern Hemisphere. I am 40,000 kilometers long!

_____

d Apples or pears, if we weigh the same, we are this!

_____

Comprehension

2 **Label the sentences L (length), W (weight), or T (time).**

a A solar year is how long it takes Earth to go around the sun. ____

b Different civilizations used different parts of the body to measure this. ____

c The definition of a Roman mile is 1,000 paces. ____

d You can ask for a pound of tomatoes in the United States. ____

3 **Correct the sentences.**

a The King of Egypt used meters to measure the pyramids of Giza.

_____

b The Mayan calendar had a larger error than modern calendars.

_____

4 **Circle the points the author does _not_ make in the conclusion on page 117.**

a Lucas had a busy day.

b Lucas can measure his day in terms of length, weight, and time.

c You could measure your day in terms of length, weight, and time, too.

d Time is the most important unit of measurement.

Digging Deeper

5 **Read and match the main points with the evidence that supports them.**

Main Points

1 In Ancient China, Emperor Qin Shi Huang decided to standardize measurements.

2 Ancient civilizations also used scales to weigh things.

3 We use calendars to keep track of time.

4 Older civilizations used a numeral system based on 12 and 60.

Evidence

a They put grains on one side and the object they wanted to weigh on the other side.

b For that reason, Egyptians divided the day into 24 parts, and the Babylonians divided one hour into 60 minutes and a minute into 60 seconds.

c He used a decimal system, so each unit was ten times bigger than the previous one.

d They measure the time it takes for the Earth to make a complete circuit around the Sun.

6 **Read the article on pages 115–117 again. Complete the graphic organizer.**

	Length	Weight	Time
a Different Units of Measurement			
b Body Parts or Equipment Used			

Personalization

7 **Measure the distance, weight, or time to answer the questions.**

1 How long can you hold your breath?

    a seconds: _____   b minutes: _____   c hours: _____

2 How far is it from one side of your classroom to the other?

    a meters: _____   b paces: _____   c cubits: _____

3 How heavy is your backpack?

    a grams: _____   b kilograms: _____   c pounds: _____

9 What makes the natural world so amazing?

Key Words

1 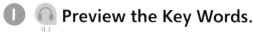 Preview the Key Words.

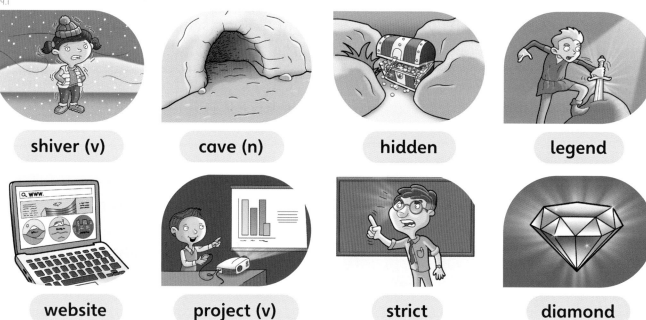

| shiver (v) | cave (n) | hidden | legend |

| website | project (v) | strict | diamond |

2 Read the definitions and write the Key Words.

a a large, natural hole in a hill or under the ground _____

b to show video, images, or text on a screen or wall _____

c a story from the past that many people believe in, even though they cannot prove it is true _____

d a group of online pages _____

Pre-reading

3 Look at the pictures on pages 121–127 and make predictions.

1	The story is about ...	a a school project.	b vacations.
2	The main characters are ...	a teachers.	b children.
3	The story takes place ...	a around the world.	b in the rainforest.
4	Everything happens ...	a in the past.	b in the present.

4 Listen and read.

The Secret of
El Dorado

By Joep van der Werff • Illustrated by Emmanuel Urueta

Noah and Chloe were getting bored. They needed a topic for a project at their school in Glasgow, Scotland, about places around the world.

"What can we do for our project?" asked Noah.

"Something about the North Pole?" suggested Chloe.

"No, thanks. I get cold even thinking about the cold there!" said Noah shivering.

"Should we talk about the pyramids in Egypt?"

"No, it's too hot there."

"And what about sharks?" asked Chloe.

"I'm afraid of them!"

Chloe took out her tablet and tapped on the keyboard a few times. Then, her eyes flashed.

"Look! Here's a BlueTube video about a mysterious place from the past. Let's watch it!"

The children saw scenes from a rainforest: tall trees shining in the sun, with leopards and monkeys. Then, the video showed images of golden treasures: statues, masks, and bars of gold.

"Hello, everybody!" said a lady dressed in an explorer's jacket and hat. "This is Madame Wildfire. In this video, I want to share a special discovery with you! Have you heard of *El Dorado*? People say this was an ancient city or a treasure made of gold. *El Dorado* means 'the golden one,' you know." Her eyes lit up and she smiled excitedly.

"Back in the 1500s and 1600s, explorers like Walter Raleigh looked for *El Dorado* in South America. But I have new, secret information. I know that Hunter Hoopla, an unknown explorer, looked for the treasures in caves around the world. This is an exclusive discovery from me, Madame Wildfire!"

She continued, "Hoopla says that *El Dorado* is not a city, but a treasure hidden in a cave. If that is true, where is it? In which cave is the treasure still hidden?"

Bank account numbers appeared on the screen. Madame Wildfire continued, "I'm doing research to find out more. Send money today and I'll provide you with more information!"

"Wow! *El Dorado* in a cave? How cool! Should we ask our parents to send the lady money?" asked Noah.

"I don't think so!" responded Chloe. "We don't know her at all. But we can talk to our teacher about making this the topic of our research project."

"That's a great idea!" agreed Noah.

"Send money NOW for more information on *El Dorado*!" the BlueTube lady was still insisting.

"Oh, I don't think so, Madame Wildfire," said Chloe and turned off her tablet. "But thanks for the great idea of *El Dorado* and the caves!"

"Chloe and I have an idea, Ms. Baldwin," Noah told their teacher. "We can investigate caves around the world to find the secret of *El Dorado*."

"Okay. Tell me more," Ms. Baldwin replied.

"Sure," said Chloe. "*El Dorado* is a famous legend. Some people believe that *El Dorado* was a man who covered himself in gold dust. Many explorers have been searching for a golden city called *El Dorado*. But we found a new report on BlueTube that *El Dorado* is in a cave, and not in South America. Noah and I would like to look into that new idea. We can ask some SchoolWorld kids to help us."

"Excellent idea, Chloe. You and Noah can work on your project with SchoolWorld," said Ms. Baldwin.

SchoolWorld was a website that allowed children from schools all over the world to communicate. Ms. Baldwin was one of the teachers who had set up projects on the site so that classes from different countries could work on them together. But first, Noah and Chloe needed to investigate some more.

Noah was watching a BlueTube video about the tropical rainforest in Colombia where the original *El Dorado* was thought to be.

"Oh boy! Look at this, Chloe. In the jungle, it's warm. You can find fruit and things to eat just in the trees. Nature will take care of you. When I grow up, I want to live there!"

But when Chloe saw the spiders and snakes that also live in the jungle, she said, "Maybe nature can take care of you, but nature can also kill you, with all these deadly animals! I prefer to live here in Scotland."

"Noah," said Chloe, "if *El Dorado* is in a cave, we can start our research in Fingal's Cave. Maybe our parents can take us there this Saturday."

"We don't have to. I went last summer!" answered Noah. "The cave is full of basalt blocks. They all have six sides, and you can walk on top of them. It's like something from a magical story. It's incredible that nature can produce those blocks by itself."

"But no gold?"

"When we walked out of the cave, it was late afternoon and we saw an incredible golden sunset. But real gold, no. I have a picture of the cave on my tablet. Here it is!"

Noah shared the picture of the cave with Ms. Baldwin and she showed it during class. Chloe and Noah called their project "The Secret of *El Dorado*." Soon they received their first response on SchoolWorld.

"What a great project!" Cameron from New Zealand said in a video. "We'd love to go to the glowworm caves for your project."

So Cameron and his class organized a school trip with their teachers and some parents. They took a long weekend to travel from their hometown of Auckland to the Waitomo Glowworm Caves. They took video clips with cell phones and sent the videos to Noah and Chloe's class. Ms. Baldwin projected one of them in the classroom.

"Here we are in a small boat. You can see me in the light of the flashlight," explained Cameron. "Now we'll turn off the light. You won't believe what you'll see next. Look!"

Once the flashlight was off, the video showed tiny spots of blue light on the walls and roof of the cave. Hundreds, no, thousands of little blue lights, like the stars shining on a beautiful clear night.

"Ooooh!" said the kids in Noah's classroom with surprise.

"That's amazing!" shouted Chloe, "What are those lights?"

As if Cameron heard the question, he answered on the video.

"These lights are completely natural. Each light is a tiny little worm called a glowworm. The worm's scientific name is ... is ..."

"*Arachnocampa luminosa*," said a girl's voice.

"Thanks, Ann. And they give off blue light. The caves were first explored by a Māori man named, named ..."

"Chief Tane Tinorau," said Ann.

"Right!" said Cameron, "Almost 150 years ago. Just imagine what they thought of the caves before there was electric light! It's not gold, but it's a miracle of Mother Nature."

"Wow, that was an incredible video," said Chloe. "I'll send Cameron a message to say thanks."

Ms. Baldwin said, "Okay, but first we have a live connection with Luis and Magda from Mexico."

Two Mexican children appeared on the screen.

"Hi, Luis! Hi, Magda! Good afternoon!" said the Scottish children.

"Hello, Scotland! Good afternoon. It's still morning here in Mexico," answered Magda. "We didn't get to the Giant Crystal Cave in Naica that we wanted to go to, though."

"That's too bad," said Noah. "Why?"

"This cave is very strange. It is very, very hot in there. Visitors need a special suit," explained Luis.

"And there are gases," added Magda.

"Yes, that's right. Toxic gases," said Luis, "so there's no way children like us can visit the caves—only scientists. They are strict about that."

"But we can show you pictures of the cave," said Magda, and she sent the pictures. Ms. Baldwin projected them.

"That cave is amazing," said Noah.

"It's more like a cave full of diamonds instead of gold!"

Later, Noah said, "*El Dorado* was not in that cave, either."

"True," said Chloe, "but there's a *natural* treasure. I was thinking that gold is worth a lot, but there are other treasures that are worth a great deal, too. Fingal's Cave, the Waitomo Glowworm Caves, and the Giant Crystal Cave are truly magical and valuable. So, I wonder, does the treasure have to be actual gold?"

"Good question!" Noah answered. "*Dorado* means golden, but there are many treasures that are not made of gold. The jungles of Colombia contain 'green gold,' Fingal's Cave has 'gray gold,' the Waitomo Glowworm Caves have 'blue gold,' and the Giant Crystal Cave is made of 'white gold,' don't you agree?"

"Yes!" shouted Chloe. "The secret of *El Dorado* is the wonderful nature that we can see all around the world!"

And then Noah said, "I was thinking about what astronauts see when they look back at the Earth from space. They are looking at the real *El Dorado*!"

"Most definitely," responded Chloe.

Key Words

1 Read the clues. Complete the crossword puzzle with the Key Words.

Across

1 My mother is very _____.
   I have to go to bed at 8 p.m.

2 She is wearing a gold ring with an
   expensive _____
   in the middle.

3 Explorers have searched everywhere
   for the _____
   treasure, but no one can find it.

Down

1 Put your jacket on before you start to _____.
   It's very cold in here!

Comprehension

2 Read and circle *T* (true) or *F* (false).

a Hunter Hoopla is a famous explorer.   T   F

b Noah visited a cave but didn't find any gold.   T   F

c Cameron's class discovered the Waitomo Glowworm Caves.   T   F

d Luis and Magda didn't go inside the Giant Crystal Cave.   T   F

e The Giant Crystal Cave has diamonds in it.   T   F

f Noah and Chloe learn more from SchoolWorld than BlueTube.   T   F

3 Write the name of the cave.

a It is dangerous and you need protective clothes. _____

b It contains rocks with six sides. _____

c You can see lights in the dark. _____

d It is in Scotland. _____

e The rocks inside the cave look like "white gold." _____

f You need to get there by boat. _____

Digging Deeper

4 📖 Read the story on pages 121–127 again. Then, complete the chart.

	Example from the Text	What We Can Guess About the Character
a Madame Wildfire's Words, Thoughts, or Actions	"'El Dorado' means 'the golden one,' you know." Her eyes lit up and she smiled excitedly.	She wants people to send money. She is greedy.
b Chloe's Words, Thoughts, or Actions		
c Noah's Words, Thoughts, or Actions		

5 📖 How are Chloe, Noah, Cameron, Luis, and Magda similar and different from Madame Wildfire? Complete.

How are the children in the story similar?	How are they different from Madame Wildfire?
_____	_____

Personalization

6 Think of natural treasures in your country. Describe your *El Dorado*.

My *El Dorado* is … _____

9 What makes the natural world so amazing?

Key Words

1 **Preview the Key Words.**
9.3

mysterious	spine	shell	camouflage (n)
mimic	predator	prey (n)	twitch (v)

2 **Read the definitions and mark (✔) the correct Key Word.**

a to move with sudden motion   ☐ shell   ☐ twitch

b to copy someone or something's behavior   ☐ mimic   ☐ spine

c strange, unknown, or difficult to understand ☐ predator   ☐ mysterious

d an animal hunted for food   ☐ prey   ☐ camouflage

Pre-reading

3 **Look at the pictures on pages 131–133. Read the statements and mark (✔).**

		Yes, I agree.	No, I disagree.	I don't know.
a	The ocean is a mysterious place.			
b	Octopuses can use tools.			
c	Octopuses are not good at hiding.			
d	Animals don't dream.			

4 **Listen and read.**
9.4

Under the Sea:
Amazing Aliens from Earth
By Robert Gareth Vaughan

a giant isopod

a red-lipped batfish

a Christmas tree worm

a tardigrade

When you look at the ocean, it doesn't look like much. It's just a lot of water. But under the ocean, it's a different story. It's a beautiful and amazing world and also a mysterious one—we don't know a lot about it. There is one thing we do know, however; it is full of incredible creatures. Look at these! From the giant isopod to the tardigrade (the strongest creature on Earth), it's like another planet!

In an ocean full of fascinating creatures, perhaps the most intriguing is one you know: the octopus. The octopus is like no other creature on Earth. In fact, it's more like something from outer space. But what makes it so unusual?

Amazing Sea Creatures
Have you ever been camping and forgotten your sleeping bag? The parrotfish don't have this problem. They make their own bed out of mucus 😮 for protection from predators.

Octopuses Are Intelligent!

Everybody knows that octopuses have eight arms and a big, round head, like a light bulb. But did you know that they have three hearts and that their blood is blue? Did you also know that they are one of the most intelligent invertebrates (animals with no spine)? They are as clever as a house cat! They are the first invertebrates to use tools. For example, some octopuses carry a coconut shell to protect themselves from predators. Other octopuses can open a jar when they are inside of one! And people who keep octopuses as pets say they have seen them watching TV from their aquariums!

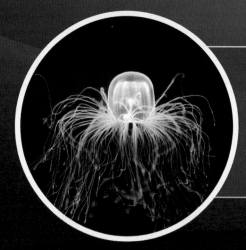

Amazing Sea Creatures

Did you know that some jellyfish can live forever? When the tiny *Turritopsis dohrnii* dies, it sinks to the bottom of the ocean. Amazingly, its cells start to re-form into simple creatures called polyps. New jellyfish grow from them!

Octopuses Are Old!

Octopuses are cephalopods, just like humans are mammals. Cephalopods means "head-foot." They were one of the first animals to hunt in our seas. They existed about 500 million years ago. This makes them older than dinosaurs!

Octopuses Are Amazing at Camouflage!

The octopus is well-known for using camouflage. This isn't unusual for some animals. But the octopus can change the way it looks very quickly—in less than one second! Amazing! An octopus can also copy, or mimic, other sea creatures. It can pretend to be a jellyfish, a crab, or a starfish. Or it can change to look like a piece of coral or rock!

Can You Find the Octopus?

Octopuses hide by using special muscles in their skin. These help the octopus mimic the same colors, patterns, and even textures as its environment. Predators like sharks and dolphins can't see them. They are also a very good predator themselves—they use their suckers and poisonous, parrot-like beak to catch their prey.

Amazing Sea Creatures

Male seahorses are the ones that get pregnant and give birth—not females! 😮 Impressive!

Dreaming Animals

Do animals dream? When your pet cat or dog twitches, or moves suddenly while sleeping, are they dreaming? It's a difficult question to answer! It would be useful if we could ask them, but we can't. However, we can observe them and look at how their brains work while they are sleeping. Scientists who have investigated this believe there is evidence to suggest that animals do dream!

This sleeping walrus may be dreaming.

We dream during the REM (Rapid Eye Movement) stage of sleep. This is when our eyes move around, and we can't move. There's a lot of electrical activity going on in the brain during this stage, too. Scientists have studied animals—dogs, cats, and reptiles—and they appear to experience REM sleep. The electrical activity in their brains is quite similar to humans. If these patterns show that humans are dreaming, then animals are probably dreaming, too.

Scientists think that octopuses probably dream, too. Recently, on the Internet, someone posted a video of an octopus named Heidi. In the video, Heidi was sleeping. While she was sleeping, she started to change color. Some scientists believe that octopuses changing color while sleeping may be similar to a cat or dog twitching while dreaming! However, scientists haven't recorded REM sleep in octopuses yet.

Do you think octopuses dream? If so, what do you think they dream about?

Key Words

1 **Unscramble the Key Words and complete the sentences.**

| h-l-e-l-s | a-u-l-c-m-o-g-f-a-e | i-n-p-e-s | r-p-r-d-e-a-t-o | c-m-i-i-m |

a _____ is something, such as color or shape, that protects an animal by making it difficult to be seen.

b A _____ kills and eats other animals.

c Some animals _____ the colors of other animals so the predators can't see them.

d A _____ protects an animal or insect. It can also cover fruit or seeds.

e The _____ is the row of connected bones down the middle of the back.

Comprehension

2 **Answer the questions.**

a **What** is the strongest creature on Earth? _____

b What does a parrotfish use to make its bed? _____

c How long can some jellyfish live? _____

d Which male marine animals get pregnant? _____

e Why do scientists think that octopuses dream? _____

f **What** do cats and dogs do when they dream? _____

3 **Circle the correct option to complete each sentence.**

a I have two / three hearts.

b My blood is red / blue!

c I can open coconuts / jars.

d I'm a cephalopod / mammal.

e My ancestors were here before / after the dinosaurs.

f I can / can't change the way I look.

g I mimic / dream about other creatures.

h My skin / beak is poisonous!

Digging Deeper

4 🗣 Underline four words you don't understand on pages 131–133. Which ones can you figure out from context? Complete the chart.

Words I Can Figure Out from Context	Words I Need to Look Up in the Dictionary
_____	_____
_____	_____

5 🗣 Choose a word from Activity 4 that you need to look up in the dictionary. Complete the chart.

a Write the word.

_____

b Is it a noun, verb, adjective, or adverb?

_____

c Look for clues in the pictures and the sentence before and after. What do you think it means?

_____

d Look it up in the dictionary. Write the meaning.

_____

Personalization

6 Complete the chart.

Dreams	Cats and Dogs	Octopuses	You
Rapid Eye Movement			
Twitching			
Change Color			

7 What do you think cats and dogs dream about? Write your ideas.

_____

_____

8 What do you dream about?

_____

_____

Acknowledgments

The authors and publishers acknowledge the following sources of copyright material and are grateful for the permissions granted. While every effort has been made, it has not always been possible to identify the sources of all the material used or to trace all copyright holders. If any omissions are brought to our notice, we will be happy to include the appropriate acknowledgments on reprinting and in the next update to the digital edition, as applicable.

Key: U = Unit.

Author of the activities: Simon Cupit.

Photographs

The following photos are sourced from Getty Images.

U1: Roger Wright/The Image Bank; Imgorthand/E+; FatCamera/E+; Brian Mitchell/Corbis Documentary; shapecharge/E+; Michael Greenberg/Photodisc; RichVintage/E+; Dave Nagel/The Image Bank; filo/DigitalVision Vectors; bubaone/DigitalVision Vectors; SDI Productions/E+; ViewStock; oxygen/Moment; katleho Seisa/E+; fstop123/E+; mikroman6/Moment; kali9/E+; Marilyn Nieves/E+; RichLegg/E+; pijama61/DigitalVision Vectors; **U2:** Filip Reznícek/EyeEm; JGI/Jamie Grill; Jasmin Merdan/Moment; stevecoleimages/E+; Stolk/iStock/Getty Images Plus; Jose A. Bernat Bacete/Moment; David Clapp/Stone; Henrik Sorensen/DigitalVision; Asim Mahmood/EyeEm; ilbusca/DigitalVision Vectors; Thinkstock Images/Stockbyte; Photos.com/PHOTOS.com>> real444/E+; Hulton Deutsch/Corbis Historical; MarioGuti/E+; Pakin Songmor/Moment; dottedhippo/iStock/Getty Images Plus; Knut Schaeffner/EyeEm; **U3:** selimaksan/E+; Richard Drury/Stone; GS Visuals/Cultura; Jesper Klausen/Science Photo Library; Kwanchai Lerttanapunyaporn/EyeEm; Jrg Weimann/EyeEm; vesi_127/Moment; Lucy Lambriex/DigitalVision; Grafissimo/DigitalVision Vectors; ZU_09/DigitalVision Vectors; EyeEm; Figula Photography/Moment Open; Dorling Kindersley; Lucy Lambriex/Moment Open; Lorado/E+; Wolfgang Weber/EyeEm; krisanapong detraphiphat/Moment; aleksandarvelasevic/DigitalVision Vectors; **U4:** Andersen Ross/DigitalVision; MarcoSchmidt.net/Moment; Sigrid Gombert/Alloy; teekid/E+; Monty Rakusen/Cultura; jamesbenet/E+; kencameron/E+; Bader-Butowski; JoseIgnacioSoto/iStock/Getty Images Plus; powerofforever/DigitalVision Vectors; Steven Robinson Pictures/Moment; Geri Lavrov/Stockbyte; da-kuk/E+; Dimitri Otis/Stone; Federica Grassi/Moment; IMAGEMORE Co, Ltd.; tacstef/iStock/Getty Images Plus; Jose Luis Pelaez Inc/DigitalVision; ilbusca/iStock Unreleased; Andrew H. Walker/Getty Images Entertainment; David Greedy/Getty Images News; Jeff Greenough; mikkelwilliam/E+; Photo by Laura Kalcheff/Moment; SDI Productions/E+; Cavan Images; CSA-Archive/DigitalVision Vectors; **U5:** Thomas M. Scheer/EyeEm; JGI/Jamie Grill; fStop Images; Westend61; bluestocking/E+; Mikolette/E+; Marilyn Nieves/E+; Dani Daniar/EyeEm; Markus Spiske/EyeEm; Ali Shah Lakhani/EyeEm; Hulton Archive; imagedepotpro/E+; Denis Goujon/EyeEm; Juan Carlos Gallego Amaya/EyeEm; Thomas M. Scheer/EyeEm; Culture Club/Hulton Archive; Paul Pirosca/EyeEm; SolStock/E+; vgajic/E+; alvarez/E+; **U6:** LauriPatterson/E+; Image Source; Ryan McVay/DigitalVision; Kateryna Kon/Science Photo Library; simon2579/DigitalVision Vectors; Phill Thornton/iStock/Getty Images Plus; dolphfyn/iStock/Getty Images Plus; zhuang wang/Moment; Chaiyun Damkaew/Moment; Pedarilhos/iStock/Getty Images Plus; mikroman6/Moment; muendo/E+; Landscapes, Seascapes, Jewellery & Action Photographer/Moment; TEK IMAGE/Science Photo Library; Wavebreakmedia/iStock/Getty Images Plus; bonchan/iStock/Getty Images Plus; Jiraroj Praditcharoenkul/iStock/Getty Images Plus; **U7:** joSon/Stone; belchonock/iStock/Getty Images Plus; KristianSeptimiusKrogh/E+; Westend61; trebuchet/iStock/Getty Images Plus; deepblue4you/E+; videophoto/E+; moodboard/Cultura; Stuart Westmorland/Corbis Documentary; Science Photo Library - NASA EARTH OBSERVATORY/Brand X Pictures; ZenShui/Frederic Cirou/PhotoAlto Agency RF Collections; John M Lund Photography Inc/DigitalVision; Maiquel Jantsch/Moment; schulzie/iStock/Getty Images Plus; Henglein and Steets/Cultura; PPAMPicture/E+; Raquel Lonas/Moment; Brett Davies - Photosightfaces/Moment; traveler1116/E+; Varadonn Buarapha/Moment Open; hadynyah/E+; **U8:** LordHenriVoton/E+; Johner Images; Blend Images - Todd Wright; Alexey Dulin/EyeEm; malerapaso/E+; Matthias Kulka/The Image Bank; Peter Dazeley/The Image Bank; ibraman3012/iStock/Getty Images Plus; FG Trade/E+; Hanis/E+; Nick Brundle Photography/Moment; Rob Shone; traveler1116/DigitalVision Vectors; Skobrik/Moment; Bernard Van Berg/EyeEm; mbbirdy/E+; Leeuwtje/E+; FotografiaBasica/E+; Géza Bálint Ujvárosi/EyeEm; Andrew_Howe/iStock/Getty Images Plus; mgkaya/E+; **U9:** yu-ji/iStock/Getty Images Plus; Westend61; Manoel Neto/EyeEm; lessydoang/RooM; Heide Benser/The Image Bank; Jean Tresfon/Moment; jared lloyd/Moment; Eric Schallow/EyeEm; Joao Paulo Burini/Moment; Hal Beral/Corbis; Mathieu Meur/Stocktrek Images; SEBASTIAN KAULITZKI/SCIENCE PHOTO LIBRARY/Science Photo Library; Alonso Romero Méndez/EyeEm; Danita Delimont; Stuart Westmorland/Corbis Documentary; Tammy616/E+; Yiming Chen/Moment; fjdelvalle/E+; Last Resort/DigitalVision; Douglas Klug/Moment Open; LuismiX/Moment; Mike Korostelev/Moment Open; CandO_Designs/DigitalVision Vectors.

U2: Courtesy of NASA.

Illustrations

Antonio Rocha; Axel Rangel; Daniela Martín del Campo; Emmanuel Urueta; Gabriela Granados; Javier Montiel; Marco Antonio Reyes; Sheila Cabeza de Vaca; Yaritza Andrade.

Cover Artwork commissioned by Aphik S.A. de C.V.

Cover Illustration by Emmanuel Urueta.

Page make-up

Aphik, S.A. de C.V.

Audio

Audio recording by CityVox.